Teri K
Horo

Cancer

**Teri King's complete horoscope
for all those whose birthdays fall
between 21 June and 22 July**

Teri King

Element
An Imprint of HarperCollins*Publishers*
77–85 Fulham Palace Road
Hammersmith, London W6 8JB

The website address is: www.thorsonselement.com

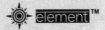

and *Element* are trademarks of
HarperCollins*Publishers* Limited

First published 2004

1

© Teri King 2004

Teri King asserts the moral right to be
identified as the author of this work

A catalogue record for this book
is available from the British Library

ISBN 0 00 718421 2

Printed and bound in Great Britain by
Clays Ltd, St Ives plc

Contents

Cancer

21 June to 22 July

Ruling Planet: **The Moon**
Element: **Water**
Quality: **Feminine**
Planetary Principle: **Love**
Primal Desire: **Security**
Colour: **Violet**
Jewel: **Emerald**
Day: **Monday**
Magical Number: **Two**

Famous Cancerians
Harrison Ford, Diana Princess of Wales,
George Michael, Jerry Hall, Courtney Love,
Johnny Depp, Camilla Parker Bowles,
Melanie Griffith, Pamela Anderson, Prince William,
Tom Hanks, Steven Spielberg, Tobey Maguire,
Robin Williams, Matt LeBlanc, Amanda Donohoe,
Tom Cruise, Ernest Hemingway, Louis Armstrong

Introduction

Astrology has many uses, not least of these is its ability to help us to understand both ourselves and other people. Unfortunately, there are many misconceptions and confusions associated with it, such as that old chestnut – how can a zodiac forecast be accurate for all the millions of people born under one particular sign?

The answer to this is that all horoscopes published in newspapers, books and magazines are, of necessity, of a general nature. Unless an astrologer can work from the date, time and place of your birth, the reading given will only be true for the typical member of your sign.

For instance, let's take a person born on 9 August. This person is principally a subject of Leo, simply because the Sun occupied that section of the heavens known as Leo during 23 July to 22 August.* However, when delving into astrology at its most serious, there are other influences that need to be taken into consideration – for example, the Moon. This planet enters a fresh sign every 48 hours. On the birth date in

* Because of the changing position of the planets, calendar dates for astrological signs change from year to year.

question it may have been in, say, Virgo. And if this were the case it would make our particular subject Leo (Sun representing willpower) and Virgo (Moon representing instincts) or, if you will, a Leo/Virgo. Then again, the rising sign of 'ascendant' must also be taken into consideration. This also changes constantly as the Earth revolves: approximately every two hours a new section of the heavens comes into view – a new sign passes over the horizon. The rising sign is of the utmost importance, determining the image projected by the subject to the outside world – in effect, the personality.

The time of birth is essential when compiling a birth chart. Let us suppose that in this particular instance Leo was rising at the time of birth. Now, because two of the three main influences are Leo, our sample case would be fairly typical of his or her sign, possessing all the faults and attributes associated with it. However, if the Moon and ascendant had been in Virgo then, whilst our subject would certainly display some of the Leo attributes or faults, it is more than likely that for the most part he or she would feel and behave more like a Virgoan.

As if life weren't complicated enough, this procedure must be carried through to take into account all the remaining planets. The position and signs of Mercury, Venus, Mars, Jupiter, Saturn, Uranus, Neptune and Pluto must all be discovered, plus the aspect formed from one planet to another. The calculation and interpretation of these movements by an astrologer will then produce an individual birth chart.

Because the heavens are constantly changing, people with identical charts are a very rare occurrence. Although it is not inconceivable that it could happen, this would mean that the two subjects were born not only on the same date and at the same time, but also in the same place. Should such an incident occur, then the deciding factors as to how these individuals would differ in their approach to life, love, career, financial prospects and so on would be due to environmental and parental influence.

Returning to our hypothetical Leo: our example, with the rising Sun in Leo and Moon in Virgo, may find it useful not only to read up on his or her Sun sign (Leo) but also to read the section dealing with Virgo (the Moon). Nevertheless, this does not invalidate Sun sign astrology. This is because of the great power the Sun possesses, and on any chart this planet plays an important role.

Belief in astrology does not necessarily mean believing in totally determined lives – that we are predestined and have no control over our fate. What it does clearly show is that our lives run in cycles, for both good and bad and, with the aid of astrology, we can make the most of, or minimize, certain patterns and tendencies. How this is done is entirely up to the individual. For example, if you are in possession of the knowledge that you are about to experience a lucky few days or weeks, then you can make the most of them by pushing ahead with plans. You can also be better prepared for illness, misfortune, romantic upset and every adversity.

Astrology should be used as it was originally intended – as a guide, especially to character. In this direction it is invaluable and it can help us in all aspects of friendship, work and romance. It makes it easier for us to see ourselves as we really are and, what's more, as others see us. We can recognize both our own weaknesses and strengths and those of others. It can give us outer confidence and inner peace.

In the following pages you will find: personality profiles; an in-depth look at the year ahead from all possible angles, including numerology; Monthly and Daily guides; and your

Sun sign partner guide – plus a brief section on your child of the Zodiac for those with children born under this sign.

Used wisely, astrology can help you through life. It is not intended to encourage complacency, since, in the final analysis, what you do with your life is up to you. This book will aid you in adopting the correct attitude to the year ahead and thus maximize your chances of success. Positive thinking is encouraged because this helps us to attract positive situations. Allow astrology to walk hand-in-hand with you and you will increase your chances of success and happiness.

How Does
Astrology Work?

You often hear people say that there is no scientific explanation of astrology. This is not a very scientific thing to say because, in fact, astrological calculations may be explained in a very precise way, and they can be done by anyone with a little practice and some knowledge of the movement of stars and planets. However, the interpretations and conclusions drawn from these observations are not necessarily consistent or verifiable, and, to be sure, predicted events do not always happen. Yet astrology has lasted in our culture for over 3,000 years, so there must be something there!

So how can we explain that astrology? Well, along with your individual birth sign goes a set of deep-seated characteristics, and an understanding of these can give you fresh insights into why you behave as you do. Reading an astrological interpretation, even if it is just to find out how, say, a new relationship might develop, means that you should think about yourself in a very deep way. But it is important to remember that the stars don't determine your fate. It is up to you to use them to the best advantage in any situation.

Although astrology, like many other 'alternative' subjects such as homoeopathy and telepathy cannot completely be explained, there have been convincing experiments to show that it is right far more often than chance would allow. The best-known studies are those of the French statistician, Michel Gauquelin, whose results were checked by a professor at the University of London who declared, grudgingly, that 'there was something in it'.

An important aspect of astrology is to look at how the Sun and the Moon affect that natural world around us, day-in day-out. For instance, the rise and fall of the tides is purely a result of the movement and position of the Moon relative to the Earth. If this massive magnetic pull can move the oceans of the Earth, what does it do to us? After all, we are, on average, over 60 per cent water!

When it comes to the ways in which the Sun may change the world, a whole book could be written about it. The influences we know about include length of day, heat, light, solar storms, and magnetic, ultra-violet and many other forms of radiation. And all this from over 90 million miles away! For example, observation of birds has shown that before migration – governed by the changing length of days – birds put on extra layers of fat, as well as experiencing a nocturnal restlessness shortly before setting off on their travels. I'm not suggesting that we put on weight and experience sleepless nights because of the time of year, but many people will tell you that different seasons affect them in different ways.

Also in the natural world, there is a curious species of giant worm that lives in underground caverns in the South Pacific. Twice a year, as the Sun is rising and the tide is at its highest, these worms come to the surface of the ocean. The inhabitants of the nearby islands consider them a great delicacy! There are so many instances where the creatures of this planet respond to the influences of the Moon and the Sun that it is only sensible to wonder whether the position of other planets also has an effect, even if it is subtler and less easy to identify.

Finally, we come to the question of how astrology might work in predicting future events. As we have seen, the planetary bodies are likely to affect us in all sorts of ways, both physically and mentally. Most often, subtle positions in the planets will make slight changes in our emotional states and, of course, this determines how we behave. By drawing up a chart based on precise birth times, and by using their intuition, some astrologers can make precise observations about how influences in the years ahead are likely to shape the life of an individual. Many people are very surprised at how well an astrologer seems to 'understand' them after reading a commentary on their birth chart!

More strange are the astrologers who appear to be able to predict future events, ages before they happen. The most famous example of all is the 16th-century French astrologer, Nostradamus, who is well known for having predicted the possibility of world destruction at the end of the last millennium. Don't worry; I think I can cheerfully put everyone's mind at rest by assuring you that the world will go on for a good many years yet. Although Nostradamus certainly made some very accurate predictions in his lifetime, his prophecies for our future are very obscure and are hotly disputed by all the experts. Mind you, it is quite clear that there are likely to be massive changes ahead. It is possible, for instance, that information may come to light about past civilizations and cities, which are now sunk beneath the Mediterranean Sea. This could give us a good idea about how people once lived, and pointers as to how we should live in the future. Try not to fear, dear reader. Astrology is a tool for us to use; if we use it wisely, no doubt we will survive with greater wisdom and with a greater respect for our world and each other.

The Sun in Cancer

You're a child of the Moon who wears your moods on your sleeve, along with a lot of longing. You are the original creature of desire and have more cravings than you or anybody else knows what to do with. You're the kind of person whom everyone needs to know and experience. You have a way of anticipating someone's needs before they happen, and of offering your unsolicited services before anyone has had the chance to ask.

Because of your super-sensitive emotional approach to others, you're a lot more vulnerable than the average person. Be careful where you place your sympathies, as people may take your generous nature for granted and tread on you when you least expect it. Such an experience is cause for an interior retreat to scrutinize your bruised and swollen sensitivities. It's more than difficult for you to detach yourself from offensive behaviour aimed in your direction and to chalk it up to someone's acid indigestion or a bad day at the office.

Others need to remember that you mean well, because everything that you do is in someone's best interest. When it comes to your own interests you crave a constant reassurance that you are loved, needed, wanted and appreciated, and that your presence produces pleasure. When you let yourself relax and enjoy your life, you have a wondrous way of making everything seem better.

In general, you are a romantic who cries at weddings, weeps over memorable moments and sniffles at sentimental movies. The problems in your own life often assume the proportions of those on stage and screen. You spend a great deal of time trying to define yourself through other people. Likewise, you allocate to others far more power over you than you ever allow yourself.

All I've got to say is that nobody's perfect, let's face it. However, you can be sensitive, kind and protective on the one hand – but you can also be harsh, moody and bad-tempered on the other. This is not surprising, as you tend to swing pendulum-like between the two extremes. If the pendulum comes to rest, it'll more than likely do so under the influence of home and family. On other aspects of the domestic side of life, of course, you cherish your marriage, but even so it has to be said you can be somewhat difficult to handle from time to time. You tend to think of other people as much as you think about yourself.

The Year Ahead:
Overview

With Pluto still moving slowly through Sagittarius, concentrating its energy in the section of your chart related to sheer hard slog, you feel as though you really deserve a break, don't you? Nevertheless, Pluto has been transforming the way you work and your relationships with your work colleagues. As this section also relates to health, you may have also begun to transform your attitude towards your own body. This trend will continue through 2005, and it will help you realize that you, too, have professional ambitions. Between 27 March and 2 September, Pluto will be in retrograde motion, and you may find yourself retracing your steps at some point. Planets in retrograde motion give you a second bite of any cherry you missed the first time round.

Meanwhile, Neptune continues to play havoc with the financial assets and responsibilities you share with someone else. Of course, the money may still be rolling in, but perhaps you have backed a few losers over the last year. It may be time for you to get a grip on your finances, as Neptune tends to confuse us all. Your kind heart may have led you to fund some rather ill-advised projects recently. While Neptune is retrograde this year, between 18 May and 26 October, there could be a stream of dreamers beating a path to your door, asking for handouts. Please try to think clearly and weigh up the pros and cons before you open your wallet.

Uranus spends all of this year in fellow water sign Pisces, and the section of your chart linked to long-distance travel, philosophy, legal matters and higher education. Uranus has a dramatic impact on our lives and some of you may be determined to go back to school, whatever age you are. You are somewhat conservative normally, but Uranus in this position is going to change your outlook radically, and you may shock your friends and family from time to time by your unorthodox attitude. Uranus also has a period of retrograde motion this year, between 14 June and 15 November, and some of your more crazy schemes may fall apart during this period. However, Uranus is going to shake up all your ideas and, generally speaking, will be a positive influence on your life if you let it.

What about Saturn? As you probably know, this is the planet that plonks obstacles down in front of us and challenges us to find a way around them. It is a somewhat restrictive influence, and as it will be in your sign until the summer, any changes you want to make could be delayed. It's helpful to remember that Saturn urges us to be realistic, and you may find certain aspects of your life that you have been clinging on to in your Cancerian way just have to go. Letting go of the past is one thing you find very hard to do, but in order to move forward it is exactly what you must do. From the beginning of the year until 21 March, Saturn will be in retrograde motion and you could be rather restless and, dare say I it, crabby! Friends and loved ones may be running for cover from time to time.

On 17 July Saturn moves into Leo for a couple of years

and, as you know, this is the section of your chart devoted to personal finances. You may have to tighten your belt a bit, especially if you have decided to swap work for study. As long as you are realistic, you'll be absolutely fine. Cancer is a thrifty sign, and I'm sure you've got a little bit of lolly stuffed under the mattress to help you through the bad times. Saturn turns retrograde on 22 November until next year.

Jupiter, bringer of opportunities, starts the year in Libra and the section of your chart devoted to your home. Whatever else is going on around you, your home life is going to be a source of comfort and joy. You may be moving this year or welcoming a new addition to your home. Jupiter turns retrograde on 2 February, and if you are taking the plunge and buying your own home or moving to a different part of the country – or a different part of the world even – there may be a few delays and setbacks that you need to work your way around. However, after Jupiter starts moving in the right direction again on 6 June, any snags will be ironed out and you'll be well on your way to domestic harmony again. Which is just the way you like it, isn't it? On 26 October Jupiter moves into Scorpio, which is another water sign like yourself. This is also the section of your chart linked to self-expression, children, sport and, best of all, romance. If you've been feeling a little lonely over the last year or so, Jupiter will bring plenty of opportunities to meet Mr or Ms Right.

Career Year

While it may be true that your sensitive nature can make you a little shy sometimes, it is not true that your career is unimportant to you. Of course, it's absolutely essential that your home life provides a secure base for you, and this may in fact be the spur that drives you on to professional success. Once you have found the career that suits you, nothing will deter you from clawing your way to the top.

You're often involved in a career that combines one of your many interests with the possibility of being rewarded financially as well. While you may appear to shy away from the limelight, you do want to be appreciated for your efforts. If this appreciation is not forthcoming, you can become a little bit resentful, can't you?

Recent planetary movements may indicate that you are even more determined to make a success of your chosen career. Cancer is often linked to the caring professions, particularly with children. Cooking and gardening are also ways of combining your passions and your profession. If you have been jogging along recently in a job that doesn't really bring you any fulfilment, you may now have decided it is time to follow your true path. Perhaps you have taken the plunge and decided to open your own restaurant, combining your love of food, your pleasure in conversation and company with your ability to make money. Maybe you have used gardening as a form of relaxation up until now but your skill and talent have led you to believe this could be your career. If you're a woman returning to work after raising a family, perhaps you could use all that you have learned to help give other kids a chance. Your intuition may lead you to try your hand at therapy or one of the New Age disciplines designed to help other people. You may even decide to learn the tarot or astrology! The truth is, whatever career you have chosen, you will treat it like your own baby. This is why you Crabs often prefer to be your own boss. That way you will have the control you want over your professional progress.

The section of your chart linked to your career is ruled by dynamic and energetic Mars. If we look at Mars's progress through the signs we can see what sort of professional changes you can make to benefit yourself and your family.

This year Mars moves in rather a strange fashion. For the first half of the year it spends just over a month in each sign it visits, but at the end of July there will be a change. As the year opens Mars is in fiery Sagittarius, which is the sheer hard slog section of your chart. You may find you've got rather a lot on your plate and your response to this depends on whether you are happy at work or feel in need of a change. If you're happy you are going to be a human dynamo; if you're miserable, you could be doing all that is humanly possible to find a new job. On 7 February, Mars moves into your opposite number of Capricorn, and you may find your partner is very helpful should you have any career matters to discuss. He or she could provide you with some new ideas and it is well worth considering them, even if at first they don't seem to be particularly relevant.

On 21 March Mars enters Aquarius, which is one of the financial sections of your chart. If debt is playing a part in keeping you stuck in a job you hate, perhaps you need to start thinking about ways of consolidating your outgoings in order to minimize them. If you're thinking of setting up your own business, please avoid the middle two weeks of April as you may find yourself living in fantasy land rather than the real world. On 1 May Mars moves into Pisces, providing you with energy and renewed belief in your own abilities. Ideas you may have been mulling over earlier in the year could get a boost now, as suddenly a window of opportunity appears for you.

While Mars is in Aries between 12 June and 27 July, you can make great strides professionally. If you're in the right job for you, there are going to be opportunities for promotion, extra responsibility and, possibly, a pay rise. If you've been looking for work unsuccessfully the perfect position may now present itself. You may be a little more assertive during this period and you could run into a few difficulties with your colleagues if you're not careful. You need to be diplomatic, and also to curb your tendency to be over-sensitive.

On 28 July Mars moves into Taurus, a compatible earth sign. This rules the networking section of your chart, and Mars remains here until the end of the year. If you're working for yourself this is a brilliant period for you to make new contacts and clients. You'll be thinking on your feet and will be able to weed out the time-wasters from the people who are really going to benefit you. Your friends are going to be a source of support and you may even find yourself going into business with one of them. Bear in mind that Mars will have a retrograde period, between 1 October and 9 December, and one or two projects may stall a little. Never forget that retrograde periods give us the opportunity to refine and restructure our plans when necessary, so learn to be flexible and you shouldn't have too many problems.

In April and again in October there will be eclipses in the sign of Aries, which rules the career section of your chart. Eclipses can be catalysts, and these may reveal a burning ambition that you didn't know you had. It is during these months that you may make important decisions related to your long-term career path and, ultimately, your personal happiness. This year could be a turning point in your professional life, so you need to be bold but also realistic.

Money Year

You find it very hard to operate at your best if you're feeling emotionally or materially insecure. To the outside world you seem to be running entirely on emotional energy, but you are quite canny where your finances are concerned. You know that lack of resources can often result in difficulties in relationships. Not only that, but it is essential for your well-being that you have a secure and comfortable home, and we all know how expensive that can be these days. While you take great pains to ensure that you are financially stable, just occasionally you will take a calculated risk. After all, your intuition is second to none and sometimes you really do know which horse is going to come in first, don't you? But it's rare to find a Cancerian who has gambled away all of his or her wealth.

You're not extravagant, but you will scrimp and save if there is something you really want. You rarely count the cost when you are spending money on the things that are important to you, perhaps a beautiful garden or more likely high-quality food. You don't consider restaurant bills as luxuries, do you? After all, enjoying delicious meals in luxurious surroundings is essential to your feelings of well-being, even if it doesn't happen very often.

It's true that you hate waste, and just occasionally you can seem to be a bit of a meanie. When it comes to your family's needs, however, you spare no expense at all.

The Sun is the planet that represents your finances, so let's have a look at its movements throughout the year to see if 2005 is going to be a struggle or a breeze. The Sun follows a very regular pattern and begins the year in your opposite sign of Capricorn. You and your partner may be putting your heads together to see exactly how you can maximize your income this year. During the middle of January you may be a little strapped for cash and have to make a few small economies, especially if you really pushed the boat out over Christmas. On 20 January, the Sun enters airy Aquarius, which is again an indication that joint financial responsibilities will be under the spotlight. At the beginning of February there could be some confusion surrounding your assets, and it is well worth a few moments of your time checking all the details with a fine-tooth comb.

On 19 February, the Sun moves into watery Pisces, and as this rules the section of your chart linked to long-distance travel, perhaps you will be booking a holiday for later in the year. You could get an unexpectedly good deal in late February. The Sun enters Aries on 21 March and career opportunities could help to boost your income. The spotlight will definitely be on your career, so it's time to show your boss exactly what you can do.

Earthy Taurus is the Sun's next stop, on 20 April. Socializing could be expensive and it's possible that you are mixing business with pleasure in order to make gains later on. Use your intuition and instincts now and you'll be laughing later in the year. The Sun drifts into airy Gemini on 21 May and this is a rather hidden section of your chart, so be very careful with your money. Your judgement may be slightly off, and other people may be less than honest too, so check your change carefully.

On 21 June, the Sun enters your own sign of Cancer, and while money might be a little tight, especially around the beginning of July, you'll be enjoying yourself so much you may not notice! On 23 July the Sun moves on into Leo and the section of your chart specifically linked to your finances. You may discover a slight discrepancy in your calculations and it's important that you tighten your belt this month, especially if you have expensive projects planned for later in the year. I know you hate to appear stingy but there are plenty of ways of enjoying life without spending too much money, especially in the summer.

On 23 August the Sun moves into Virgo and you could find a local opportunity to make a little bit extra, so keep your eyes and ears open. When the Sun drifts into Libra, on 23 September, you could be spending money on your home. If you work from home or you make or sell items linked to the home, you could find yourself doing rather well.

The Sun enters fellow water sign Scorpio on 23 October, and if you have been thrifty during the summer you'll be very glad now, as the prospects for socializing look thrilling. You may have to splash out on some new clothes so that you look your best. If you're creative you could spot a sudden opportunity to market your work. On 22 November the Sun moves into Sagittarius, the sheer hard slog section of your chart. If you feel you are not being rewarded adequately for all your hard work, you may become a little resentful and it's worth thinking about your own attitude. It's true that our beliefs about ourselves are reflected back to us by the world and, if deep down inside you don't feel you deserve to be rewarded, that's what tends to happen. Repeat the phrase 'Because I'm worth it' over and over again to yourself until you really believe it. You'll find that others start to respond positively!

As the year draws to a close, the Sun moves back into your opposite number Capricorn on 22 December. I'm sure you'll be focusing all your attention on your loved ones, and no doubt you will spend lots of money on making them happy.

Love and Sex Year

In order to feel really secure, Crabs like to be in a settled relationship. In fact, so important is this to you that you may hang on to your partner for dear life, even if he or she is not making you very happy. Despite your reserved and somewhat touchy exterior, you have a very soft centre and when you fall in love, you will do almost anything to protect and maintain your relationship. Most of the time your partner appreciates you fussing over him or her, but sometimes you can be a little too clingy. Everyone, even you, needs space from time to time. Unfortunately, if your loved ones snaps at you, you take it very much to heart, don't you? What's more, you take a very long time to get over real or imagined slights.

While you may often take the role of protector within your relationship, what you really want is someone to take care of you. No matter what you do or who you are, when it comes to love, you are ruled entirely by your feelings. You need reassurance and plenty of affection, and you're happy to give both in turn. However any sign of rejection from your loved one and you will withdraw into that famous shell. You're not likely to complain loudly if your partner is not living up to your expectations, but what you will do is sulk and drop plenty of hints that his or her behaviour just isn't on.

Loyalty is a quality you prize and yours is never in question. It takes a great deal before you will break up an important relationship or a marriage, possibly to the detriment of yourself. Even though your head may tell you it's more sensible to walk away, your heart is whispering that you should stay. Nonetheless there sometimes comes a time when even you may have to face reality and call it a day.

A footloose and fancy-free Crab is a delightful companion, and some of you may enjoy playing the field before you finally put down roots. But it's probably true to say that many of you believe that a committed relationship, a home and a family are your true goals.

As your opposite number is Capricorn, Saturn is the ruler of the relationship section in your chart. Saturn represents stability, security and also reality. Saturn itself is currently in your own sign, and will be there until 15 July. This is a somewhat difficult position for you, as any cracks in your current relationship will be getting bigger and even you will be unable to ignore them. Sadly, some of you may find yourself back out there in the singles market this year if, despite your most tenacious efforts, your relationship does eventually come to an end. If you are suddenly single again, try not to slip into that Cancerian habit of living in the past. There are going to be plenty of opportunities this year to meet somebody new who may in fact turn out to be that special someone, your soul mate.

While Saturn rules relationships for you, we can't ignore the influence of Venus, the planet that rules love and relationships in general. Let's have a look at Venus's movements through the Zodiac in 2005 and see when you're most likely to meet someone special.

Venus begins the year in Sagittarius, and co-workers will be friendly and could also be instrumental in introducing you to someone new. On 10 January Venus moves into Capricorn, your opposite number. This is the time to make sure you're looking your best and feeling confident. If you are settled with your partner, this could be a particularly loving phase, as you seem to be very in tune with each other.

On 3 February Venus enters Aquarius and you may be too busy concentrating on your financial situation to pay much attention to your love life. This is a shame because you will be particularly alluring at this time. On 26 February Venus enters Pisces, a watery, emotional and romantic sign like you. You may find yourself attracted to someone with a very different background or outlook to your own. This is intriguing but may not in the long run lead to a serious relationship.

On 23 March Venus enters Aries, and an office romance is not out of the question. Bear in mind your other half, if you have one, may complain that you are spending too much time at work. So do try to reassure him or her that there is nothing to worry about, won't you? Venus enters Taurus on 16 April, which is a social section in your chart. Single Crabs should be on the lookout for plenty of opportunities to make an impression. From 10 May until 3 June, Venus is hidden away in Gemini and, unless you are involved in a secret affair, you may prefer a little solitude during this period. When Venus enters your own sign, on 4 June, you are again ready to dazzle the opposite sex. If you meet someone towards the end of the month, it could turn out be a long-term liaison.

Venus moves into Leo on 28 June, which, as you know, is a financial section in your chart. You might be spending money trying to impress someone, but really you should just rely on your own charm. On 23 July Venus moves to Virgo and love may come when you least expect it, perhaps while waiting for a bus or shopping at the local supermarket. A brother or sister may introduce you to a charming stranger, so don't turn down any invitations, however boring they might seem at first. When Venus enters Libra on 17 August, your home life will be very attractive to you. Perhaps you've just moved in with your lover and are enjoying decorating your home and choosing furniture and knick-knacks. If you share a house or flat with friends, one of them may introduce you to someone new.

On 12 September Venus moves into Scorpio and this is a wonderful period for you whether you are single or attached. You are at your most charming, witty and endearing and no one can resist you when you're on this kind of form. Make the most of it if you're looking for Mr or Ms Right.

While Venus is in Sagittarius, from 8 October until 4 November, the work front is where you might be enjoying a light flirtation. This could get serious towards the end of October, so if you think you might get your fingers burned you'd better slither out of it quickly. On 5 November Venus enters your opposite number, Capricorn, and relationships with everyone, serious or casual, will be delightful. It's a wonderful period for you and the chances of spending the holiday season on your own are very slim indeed. Venus moves into Aquarius on 16 December and if you are still feeling lonely, I'll let you into a little secret: next year Venus moves back into Capricorn for an extended stay. So, Cancer, you have plenty to look forward to, I think you'll agree.

Health and Diet Year

There is no doubt about it, Cancer you do love your food, don't you? And as you are probably a complete stranger to the gym, you may have put on a little bit of weight over the festive season. Never mind, with Saturn in Cancer for the first half of this year, you should have the discipline required to get back in trim. Your talent for cooking ensures that you can make delicious meals that aren't laden with calories. Make sure that you get plenty of roughage in the form of fresh fruit and vegetables and you won't go far wrong.

You are ruled by the Moon, Cancer, and water is very important to your health and well-being. You may avoid drinking too much as you have a tendency to retain fluid, but paradoxically, drinking plenty of plain water helps to kick-start the elimination processes within your body.

Your sensitivity and intuitive nature can mean that you pick up undercurrents in the atmosphere and absorb them yourself. This can mean you feel under the weather if you're around angry people or unpleasant situations. Obviously you can't avoid this sort of thing all the time, but you can learn to protect yourself by creating your own boundaries. Your sign rules the stomach and I'm sure you are well aware that when you have an argument or are upset, your stomach reacts badly, possibly leading to constipation or its opposite.

While Pluto, the planet of transformation, is in Sagittarius all year and the section of your chart linked to your health, you may be looking at your lifestyle with a very critical eye. It's true that everyone feels the need to detox in January, but how many of us are still leading a healthy lifestyle by the end of the following December? Pluto will help give you the determination you need to overhaul your bad habits and improve your health.

Venus is also an important planet where health matters are concerned. In January Venus is in Sagittarius for a week and you may still be hoovering up left-over chocolate and booze from Christmas. On 10 January Venus moves into Capricorn, and you may suddenly realize your favourite clothes are just a little bit too tight. As this is also a very sociable placing, it may be the spur you need to lose a few pounds.

While Venus is in Aquarius, from 3 February until the 25th, you may find yourself more fascinated by the calorific content and chemical make-up of food rather than its taste. Venus enters Pisces on 26 February and thoughts of summer holidays may spur you on if you've begun to lose interest in your fitness regime. On 23 March Venus will whiz into fiery Aries and you want to be looking good to take advantage of all those career opportunities, don't you? Venus moves on into Taurus on 16 April, which again is a very sociable section in your chart. You may overdo the rich food now as you're definitely going to be out and about more than usual.

While Venus is in Gemini, from 10 May until 3 June, you could be susceptible to all the bugs and viruses going around, and you'll need to stock up on the vitamins if you are going to avoid them. Between the 4th and 27th Venus is in your own sign, and all that hard work will have paid off. You'll be feeling absolutely fabulous and looking wonderful as well. Just in time for the summer! You certainly won't be hiding under a towel on the beach, will you?

Venus enters Leo on 28 June and you could get rather stressed out if you have complex money matters to attend to. Perhaps it will be helpful to develop a way of calming yourself down. If you've never tried meditation or yoga, it might be a good time to start.

When Venus is in Virgo, between 23 July and 16 August, you will probably be spending plenty of time with your close family. If there are any children around, you could pick up one of their little infections, so do take care, won't you? If you're not careful, joining in with their games could lead to one or two cuts and bruises as well. Venus enters Libra on 17 August and your home life will take up a lot of your time and attention. Be very careful if you are making any minor home improvements, as you could be a bit too ambitious with the DIY and have a small accident.

From 12 September until 7 October, Venus is in sexy Scorpio. I'm sure you will be enjoying yourself so much that food and drink may be way down on your list of priorities. Should you be a sporty Cancerian, take care, as you may be tempted to push yourself too far.

Venus is back in Sagittarius on 8 October, and as this is the greedy pig section of your chart, you need to be careful. After all, you are what you eat, aren't you? You don't want to undo all your hard work. From 5 November until 15 December, Venus is in your opposite sign of Capricorn and you'll probably be wining and dining with your loved one. You may not be interested in counting calories now that love is on the menu. When Venus moves into Aquarius, on 16 December, you can relax and enjoy the holiday season with your family and friends.

Numerology Year

In order to discover the number of any year you are interested in, your 'individual year number', first take your birth date, day and month, and add this to the year you are interested in, be it in the past or in the future. As an example, say you were born on 13 August and the year you are interested in is 2005:

$$
\begin{array}{r}
13 \\
+ \quad 8 \\
+ \quad 2005 \\
\hline
2026
\end{array}
$$

Then, write down 2 + 0 + 2 + 6 and you will discover this equals 10. If you add these two digits together the total is 1. This means that your year number is 1. You can experiment with this method by taking any year from your past and following this guide to find whether or not numerology works out for you.

The guide is perennial and applicable to all Sun signs: you can look up years for your friends as well as for yourself. Use it to discover general trends ahead, the way you should be approaching a chosen period and how you can make the most of the future.

Individual Year Number 1

General Feel

A time for being more self-sufficient and one when you should be ready to really go for it. All opportunities must be snapped up, after careful consideration. Also an excellent time for laying down the foundations for future success in all areas.

Definition

Because this is the number 1 individual year, you will have the chance to start again in many areas of life. The emphasis will be upon the new; there will be fresh faces in your life, more opportunities and perhaps even new experiences. If you were born on the 1st, 19th or 28th and were born under the sign of Aries or Leo, then this will be an extremely important time. It is crucial during this cycle that you be prepared to go it alone, push back horizons and generally open up your mind. Time also for playing the leader or pioneer wherever necessary. If you have a hobby which you wish to turn into a business, or maybe you simply wish to introduce other people to your ideas and plans, then do so whilst experiencing this individual cycle. A great period too for laying down plans for long-term future gains. Therefore, make sure you do your homework well and you will reap the rewards at a later date.

Relationships

This is an ideal period for forming new bonds, perhaps business relationships, new friends and new loves, too. You will be attracted to those in high positions and with strong personalities. There may also be an emphasis on bonding with people a good deal younger than yourself. If you are already in a long-standing relationship, then it is time to clear away the dead wood between you which may have been causing misunderstandings and unhappiness. Whether in love or business, you will find those who are born under the sign of Aries, Leo or Aquarius far more common in your life, also those born on the following dates: 1st, 4th, 9th, 10th, 13th, 18th, 19th, 22nd and 28th. The most important months for this individual year, when you are likely to meet up with those who have a strong influence on you, are January, May, July and October.

Career

It is likely that you have been wanting to break free and to explore fresh horizons in your career, and this is definitely a year for doing so. Because you are in a fighting mood, and because your decision-making qualities as well as your leadership qualities are foremost, it will be an easy matter for you to find assistance as well as to impress other people. Major professional changes are likely and you will also feel more independent within your existing job. Should you want times for making important career moves, then choose Mondays or Tuesdays. These are good days for pushing your luck and presenting your ideas well. Changes connected with your career are going to be more likely during April, May, July and September.

Health

If you have forgotten the name of your doctor or dentist, then this is the year to start regular check-ups. A time too when people of a certain age are likely to start wearing glasses. The

emphasis seems to be on the eyes. Start a good health regime.
This will help you cope with any adverse events that almost
assuredly lie ahead. The important months for your own
health as well as for loved ones are March, May and August.

Individual Year Number 2

General Feel
You will find it far easier to relate to other people.

Definition
What you will need during this cycle is diplomacy, co-
operation and the ability to put yourself in someone else's
shoes. Whatever you began last year will now begin to show
signs of progress. However, don't expect miracles; changes
are going to be slow rather than at the speed of light. Changes
will be taking place all around you. It is possible, too, that you
will be considering moving from one area to another, maybe
even to another country. There is a lively feel about domesticity and in relationships with the opposite sex, too. This is
going to be a marvellous year for making things come true
and asking for favours. However, on no account should you
force yourself and your opinions on other people. A spoonful
of honey is going to get you a good deal further than a spoonful of vinegar. If you are born under the signs of Cancer or
Taurus, or if your birthday falls on the 2nd, 11th, 20th or 29th,
then this year is going to be full of major events.

Relationships
You need to associate with other people far more than is usually the case – perhaps out of necessity. The emphasis is on
love, friendship and professional partnerships. The opposite

sex will be much more prepared to get involved in your life than is normally the case. This year you have a far greater chance of becoming engaged or married, and there is likely to be a lovely addition both to your family and to the families of your friends and those closest to you. The instinctive and caring side of your personality is going to be very strong and very obvious. You will quickly discover that you will be particularly touchy and sensitive to things that other people say. Further, you will find those born under the signs of Cancer, Taurus and Libra entering your life far more than is usually the case. This also applies to those who are born on the 2nd, 6th, 7th, 11th, 15th, 20th, 24th, 25th or 29th of the month.

Romantic and family events are likely to be emphasized during April, June and September.

Career

There is a strong theme of change here, but there is no point in having a panic attack about that because, after all, life is about change. However, in this particular individual year any transformation or upheaval is likely to be of an internal nature, such as at your place of work, rather than external. You may find your company is moving from one area to another, or perhaps there are changes between departments. Quite obviously, then, the most important thing for you to do in order to make your life easy is to be adaptable. There is a strong possibility, too, that you may be given added responsibility. Do not flinch, as this will bring in extra reward.

If you are thinking of searching for employment this year, then try to arrange all meetings and negotiations on Mondays or Fridays. These are good days for asking for favours or rises, too. The best months are March, April, June, August and December. All these are important times for change.

Health

This individual cycle emphasizes stomach problems. The important thing for you is to eat sensibly, rather than go on a crash diet, for example – this could be detrimental. If you are female then you would be wise to have a check-up at least once during the year ahead just to be sure you can continue to enjoy good health. All should be discriminating when dining out. Check cutlery, and take care that food has not been only partially cooked. Furthermore, emotional stress could get you down, but only if you allow it. Provided you set aside some periods of relaxation in each day when you can close your eyes and let everything drift away, you will have little to worry about. When it comes to diet, be sure that the emphasis is on nutrition, rather than fighting the flab. Perhaps it would be a good idea to become less weight-conscious during this period and let your body find its natural ideal weight on its own. The months of February, April, July and November may show health changes in some way. Common sense is your best guide during this year.

Individual Year Number 3

General Feel

You are going to be at your most creative and imaginative during this time. There is a theme of expansion and growth and you will want to polish up your self-image in order to make the 'big impression'.

Definition

It is a good year for reaching out, for expansion. Social and artistic developments should be interesting as well as profitable, and this will help to promote happiness. There will be a strong urge in you to improve yourself – either your image, your reputation or, perhaps, your mind. Your popularity soars through the ceiling, and this delights you. Involving yourself with something creative brings increased success plus a good deal of satisfaction. However, it is imperative that you keep yourself in a positive mood. This will attract attention and appreciation of all your talents. Projects which were begun two years ago are likely to be bearing fruit this year. If you are born under the signs of Pisces or Sagittarius, or your birthday falls on the 3rd, 12th, 21st or 30th, then this year is going to be particularly special and successful.

Relationships

There is a happy-go-lucky feel about all your relationships and you are in a flirty, fancy-free mood. Heaven help anyone trying to catch you during the next 12 months: they will need to get their skates on. Relationships are likely to be light-hearted and fun rather than heavy-going. It is possible, too, that you will find yourself with those who are younger than you, particularly those born under the signs of Pisces and Sagittarius, and those whose birth dates add up to 3, 6 or 9. Your individual cycle shows important months for relation-ships are March, May, August and December.

Career

As I discussed earlier, this individual number is one that suggests branching out and personal growth, so be ready to take on anything new. Not surprisingly, your career prospects look bright and shiny. You are definitely going to be more ambi-tious and must keep up that positive façade and attract opportunities. Avoid taking obligations too lightly; it is important that you adopt a conscientious approach to all your responsibilities. You may take on a fresh course of learning or look for a new job, and the important days for doing so would be Thursdays and Fridays: these are definitely your best days. This is particularly true in the months of February, March, May, July and November: expect expansion in your life and take a chance during these times.

Health

Because you are likely to be out and about painting the town all the colours of the rainbow, it is likely that health problems could come through over-indulgence or perhaps tiredness. However, if you must have some health problems, I suppose these are the best ones to experience, because they are under your control. There is also a possibility that you may get a little fraught over work, which may result in some emotional scenes. However, you are sensible enough to realize they should not be taken too seriously. If you are prone to skin allergies, then these too could be giving you problems during this particular year. The best advice you can follow is not to go to extremes that will affect your body or your mind. It is all very well to have fun, but after a while too much of it affects not only your health but also the degree of enjoyment you experience. Take extra care between January and March, and June and October, especially where these are winter months for you.

Individual Year Number 4

General Feel

It is back to basics this year. Do not build on shaky foundations. Get yourself organized and be prepared to work a little harder than you usually do and you will come through without any great difficulty.

Definition

It is imperative that you have a grand plan. Do not simply
rush off without considering the consequences, and avoid
dabbling of any kind. It is likely, too, that you will be gather-
ing more responsibility, and on occasions this could lead you
to feeling unappreciated, claustrophobic and perhaps over-
burdened in some ways. Although it is true to say that this
cycle in your individual life tends to bring about a certain
amount of limitation, whether this be on the personal, psy-
chological or financial side of life, you now have the chance to
get yourself together and to build on more solid foundations.
Security is definitely your key word at this time. When it
comes to any project, job or plan, it is important that you ask
the right questions. In other words, do your homework and
do not rush blindly into anything. That would be a disaster. If
you are an Aquarius, a Leo or a Gemini, or you were born on
the 4th, 13th, 22nd or the 31st of any month, this individual
year will be extremely important and long remembered.

Relationships

You will find that it is the eccentric, the unusual, the uncon-
ventional and the downright odd that will be drawn into your
life during this particular cycle. It is also strongly possible that
people you have not met for some time may be re-entering
your circle, and an older person or somebody outside your
own social or perhaps religious background will be drawn to
you, too. When it comes to the romantic side of life, again you
are drawn to that which is different from usual. You may even
form a relationship with someone who comes from a totally
different background, perhaps from far away. Something
unusual about them stimulates and excites you. Gemini, Leo
and Aquarius are your likely favourites, as well as anyone

whose birth number adds up to 1, 4, 5 or 7. Certainly the most exciting months for romance are going to be February, April, July and November. Make sure then that you socialize a lot during these particular times, and be ready for literally anything.

Career

Once more we have the theme of the unusual and different in this area of life. You may be plodding along in the same old rut when suddenly lightning strikes and you find yourself besieged by offers from other people and in a panic, not quite sure what to do. There may be a period when nothing particular seems to be going on when, to your astonishment, you are given a promotion or some exciting challenge. Literally anything can happen in this particular cycle of your life. The individual year 4 also inclines towards added responsibilities – it is important that you do not off-load them onto other people or cringe in fear. They will eventually pay off and, in the meantime, you will be gaining in experience and paving the way for greater success in the future. When you want to arrange any kind of meeting, negotiation or perhaps ask for a favour at work, then try to do so on a Monday or a Wednesday for the luckiest results. January, February, April, October and November are certainly the months when you must play the opportunist and be ready to say 'yes' to anything that comes your way.

Health

The biggest problems that you will have to face this year are caused by stress, so it is important that you attend to your diet and take life as philosophically as possible, as well as being ready to adapt to changing conditions. You are likely to find that people you thought you knew well are acting out of character and this throws you off-balance. Take care, too, when visiting the doctor. Remember that you are dealing with a human being and that doctors, like the rest of us, can make mistakes. Unless you are 100 per cent satisfied, go for a second opinion over anything important. Try to be sceptical about yourself because you are going to be a good deal more moody than usual. The times that need special attention are February, May, September and November. If any of these months falls in the winter part of your year, then wrap up well and dose up on vitamin C.

Individual Year Number 5

General Feel
There will be many more opportunities for you to get out and about, and travel is certainly going to be playing a large part in your year. Change, too, must be expected and even embraced – after all, it is part of life. You will have more free time and choices, so all in all things look promising.

Definition
It is possible that you tried previously to get something off the launchpad, but for one reason or another it simply didn't happen. Luckily, you now get a chance to renew those old plans and put them into action. You are certainly going to feel that things are changing for the better in all areas. You will be more actively involved with the public and enjoy a certain amount of attention and publicity. You may have failed in the past, but this year mistakes will be easier to accept and learn from; you are going to find yourself both physically and men-tally more in tune with your environment and with those you

care about than ever before. If you are a Gemini or a Virgo, or were born on the 5th, 14th or 23rd, then this is going to be a period of major importance for you and you must be ready to take advantage of this.

Relationships

Lucky you! Your sexual magnetism goes through the ceiling and you will be involved in many relationships during the year ahead. You have that extra charisma about you which will be attracting others and you can look forward to being choosy. There will be an inclination to be drawn to those who are considerably younger than yourself. It is likely, too, that you will find that those born under the signs of Taurus, Gemini, Virgo and Libra, as well as those whose birth date adds up to 2, 5 or 6, will play an important part in your year. The months for attracting others in a big way are January, March, June, October and December.

Career

This is considered by all numerologists as being one of the best numbers for self-improvement in all areas, but particularly on the professional front. It will be relatively easy for you to sell your ideas and yourself, as well as to push your skills and expertise under the noses of other people. They will certainly sit up and take notice. Clearly, then, this is a time for you to view the world as your oyster and to get out there and grab your piece of the action. You have increased confidence and should be able to get exactly what you want. Fridays and Wednesdays are perhaps the best days if looking for a job or going to negotiations or interviews, or in fact for generally pushing yourself into the limelight. Watch out for March, May, September, October or December. Something of great importance could pop up at this time. There will certainly be a chance for advancement; whether you take it or not is, of course, entirely up to you.

Health
Getting a good night's rest could be your problem during the year ahead, since that mind of yours is positively buzzing and won't let you rest. Try turning your brain off at bedtime, otherwise you will finish up irritable and exhausted. Try to take things one step at a time without rushing around. Meditation may help you to relax and do more for your physical well-being than anything else. Because this is an extremely active year, you will need to do some careful planning so that you can cope with ease rather than rushing around like a demented mayfly. Furthermore, try to avoid going over the top with alcohol, food, sex, gambling or anything that could be described as a 'quick fix'. During January, April, August and October watch yourself a bit; you could do with some pampering, particularly if any of these happen to be winter months for you.

Individual Year Number 6

General Feel
There is likely to be increased responsibility and activity within your domestic life. There will be many occasions when you will be helping loved ones, and your sense of duty is going to be strong.

Definition
Activities for the most part are likely to be centred around property, family, loved ones, romance and your home. Your artistic appreciation will be good and you will be drawn to

anything that is colourful and beautiful, and possessions that have a strong appeal to your eye or even your ear. Where domesticity is concerned, there is a strong suggestion that you may move out of one home into another. This is an excellent time, too, for self-education, for branching out, for graduating, for taking on some extra courses – whether simply to improve your prospects or improve your mind. When it comes to your social life you are inundated with chances to attend events. You are going to be a real social butterfly, flitting from scene to scene and enjoying yourself thoroughly. Try to accept nine out of ten invitations that come your way, because they bring with them chances of advancement. If you are born on the 6th, 15th or 24th, or should your birth sign be Taurus, Libra or Cancer, then this year will be long remembered as a very positive one.

Relationships

When it comes to love, sex and romance, the individual year 6 is perhaps the most successful. It is a time for being swept off your feet, for becoming engaged or even getting married. On the more negative side, perhaps, there could be separation and divorce. However, the latter can be avoided, provided you are prepared to sit down and communicate properly. There is an emphasis, too, on pregnancy and birth, or changes in existing relationships. Circumstances will be sweeping you along. If you are born under the sign of Taurus, Cancer or Libra, then it is even more likely that this will be a major year for you, as well as for those born on dates adding up to 6, 3 or 2. The most memorable months of your year are going to be February, May, September and November. Grab all opportunities to enjoy yourself and improve your relationships during these periods.

Career

A good year for this side of life, too, with the chances of promotion and recognition for past efforts all coming your way.
You will be able to improve your position in life even though
it is likely that recently you have been disappointed. On the
cash front, big rewards will come flooding in, mainly because
you are prepared to fulfil your obligations and commitments
without complaint or protest. Other people will appreciate all
the efforts you have put in, so plod along and you will find
your efforts will not have been in vain. If you are looking for a
job or setting up an interview, negotiation or a meeting, or
simply want to advertise your talents in some way, then your
best days for doing so are Mondays, Thursdays and Fridays.
Long-term opportunities are very strong during the months
of February, April, August, September and November. These
are the key periods for pushing yourself up the ladder of
success.

Health

If you are to experience any problems of a physical nature
during this year, then they could be tied up with the throat,
nose or the tonsils, plus the upper parts of the body. Basically,
what you need to stay healthy during this year is plenty of
sunlight, moderate exercise, fresh air and changes of scene.
Escape to the coast if this is at all possible. The months for
being particularly watchful are March, July, September and
December. Think twice before doing anything during these
times and there is no reason why you shouldn't stay hale and
hearty for the whole year.

Individual Year Number 7

General Feel

A year for inner growth and for finding out what really makes
you tick and what you need to make you happy. Self-awareness
and discovery are all emphasized during the individual year 7.

Definition

You will be provided with the opportunity to place as much
emphasis as possible on your personal life and your own
well-being. There will be many occasions when you will find
yourself analysing your past motives and actions, and giving
more attention to your own personal needs, goals and desires.
There will also be many occasions when you will want to
escape any kind of confusion, muddle or noise; time spent
alone will not be wasted. This will give you the chance to
meditate and also to examine exactly where you have come to
so far, and where you want to go in the future. It is important
that you make up your mind about what you want out of this
particular year, because once you have done so you will attain
those ambitions. Failure to do this could mean you end up
chasing your own tail, and that is a pure waste of time and
energy. You will also discover that secrets about yourself and
other people could be surfacing during this year. If you are
born under the sign of Pisces or Cancer, or on the 7th, 16th or
25th, then this year will be especially wonderful.

Relationships

It has to be said from the word go that this is not the best year
for romantic interest. A strong need for contemplation will
mean spending time on your own. Any romance that does
develop this year may not live up to your expectations, but,

provided you are prepared to take things as they come without jumping to conclusions, then you will enjoy yourself without getting hurt. Decide exactly what it is you have in mind and then go for it. Romantic interests this year are likely to be with people who are born on dates that add up to 2, 4 or 7, or with people born under the sign of Cancer or Pisces. Watch for romantic opportunities during January, April, August and October.

Career

When we pass through this particular individual cycle, two things in life tend to occur: retirement from the limelight and a general slowing down, perhaps by taking leave of absence or maybe retraining in some way. It is likely, too, that you will become more aware of your own occupational expertise and skills – you will begin to understand your true purpose in life and will feel much more enlightened. Long-sought-after goals begin to come to life if you have been drifting of late. The best attitude to have throughout this year is an exploratory one when it comes to your work. If you want to set up negotiations, interviews or meetings, arrange them for Mondays or Fridays. In fact, any favours you seek should be tackled on these days. January, March, July, August, October and December are particularly good for self-advancement.

Health

Since in comparison with previous years this is a rather quiet time, health problems are likely to be minor. Some will possibly arise through irritation or worry, and the best thing to do is to attempt to remain meditative and calm. This state of mind will bring positive results. Failure to do so may create unnecessary problems by allowing your imagination to run completely out of control. You need time this year to restore, recuperate and contemplate. Any health changes that do occur are likely to happen in February, June, August and November.

Individual Year Number 8

General Feel

This is going to be a time for success, for making important moves and changes, a time when you may gain power and certainly one when your talents are going to be recognized.

Definition

This individual year gives you the chance to 'think big'; it is a time when you can occupy the limelight and wield power. If you were born on the 8th, 17th or 26th of the month, or come under the sign of Capricorn, pay attention to this year and make sure you make the most of it. You should develop greater maturity and discover a true feeling of faith and destiny, both in yourself and in events that occur. This part of the cycle is connected with career, ambition and money, but debts from the past will have to be repaid. For example, an old responsibility or debt that you may have avoided in past years may reappear to haunt you. However, whatever you do with these 12 months, aim high – think big, think success and, above all, be positive.

Relationships

This particular individual year is one which is strongly connected with birth, divorce and marriage – most of the landmarks we experience in life, in fact. Love-wise, those who are more experienced or older than you, or people of power, authority, influence or wealth, will be very attractive. This year

will be putting you back in touch with those from your past –
old friends, comrades, associates and even romances from
long ago crop up once more. You should not experience any
great problems romantically this year, especially if you are
dealing with Capricorns or Librans, or with those whose date
of birth adds up to 8, 6 or 3. The best months for romance to
develop are likely to be March, July, September and December.

Career

The number 8 year is generally believed to be the best one
when it comes to bringing in cash. It is also good for asking
for a rise or achieving promotion or authority over other
people. This is your year for basking in the limelight of success, the result perhaps of your past efforts. Now you will be
rewarded. Financial success is all but guaranteed, provided
you keep faith with your ambitions and yourself. It is important that you set major goals for yourself and work slowly
towards them. You will be surprised how easily they are fulfilled. Conversely, if you are looking for work, then do set up
interviews, negotiations and meetings, preferably on Satur-
days, Thursdays or Fridays, which are your luckiest days.
Also watch out for chances to do yourself a bit of good during
February, June, July, September and November.

Health

You can avoid most health problems, particularly headaches,
constipation or liver problems, by avoiding depression and
feelings of loneliness. It is important when these descend that
you keep yourself busy enough not to dwell on them. When it
comes to receiving attention from the medical profession, you
would be well advised to get a second opinion. Eat wisely
and try to keep a positive and enthusiastic outlook on life,

and all will be well. Periods which need special care are January, May, July and October. Therefore, if any of these months fall during the winter part of your year, wrap up well and dose yourself with vitamins.

Individual Year Number 9

General Feel
A time for tying up loose ends. Wishes are likely to be fulfilled and matters brought to swift conclusions. Inspiration runs amok. Much travel is likely.

Definition
The number 9 individual year is perhaps the most successful of all. It tends to represent the completion of matters and affairs, whether in work, business or personal affairs. Your ability to let go of habits, people and negative circumstances or situations that may have been holding you back is strong. The sympathetic and humane side of your character also surfaces and you learn to give more freely of yourself without expecting anything in return. Any good deeds that you do will certainly be well rewarded in terms of satisfaction, and perhaps financially, too. If you are born under the sign of Aries or Scorpio, or on the 9th, 18th or 27th of the month, this is certainly going to be an all-important year.

Relationships
The individual year 9 is a cycle that gives appeal as well as influence. Because of this, you will be getting emotionally tied up with members of the opposite sex who may be outside your usual cultural or ethnic group. The reason for this is that this particular number relates to humanity and, of course, this

tends to quash ignorance, pride and bigotry. You also discover that Aries, Leo and Scorpio people are going to be much more evident in your domestic affairs, as well as those whose birth dates add up to 9, 3 or 1. The important months for relationships are February, June, August and November. These will be extremely hectic and eventful from a romantic viewpoint, and there are times when you could be swept off your feet.

Career

This is a year that will help to make many of your dreams and ambitions come true. Furthermore, it is an excellent time for success if you are involved in marketing your skills, talents and expertise more widely. You may be thinking of expanding abroad, for example – if so, this is certainly a good idea. You will find that harmony and co-operation with your fellow workers are easier than before, and this will help your dreams and ambitions. The best days for you if you want to line up meetings or negotiations are going to be Tuesdays and Thursdays, and this also applies if you are looking for employment or want a special day for doing something of an ambitious nature. Employment or business changes could also feature during January, May, June, August and October.

Health

The only physical problems you may have during this particular year will be because of accidents, so be careful. Try, too, to avoid unnecessary tension and arguments with other people. Take extra care when you are on the roads: no drinking and driving, for example. You will only have problems if you play your own worst enemy. Be extra careful when in the kitchen or bathroom: sharp instruments that you find in these areas can lead to cuts, unless you take care.

Your Sun Sign Partner

Cancer with Cancer

You are a cosy couple who probably never leave the house when you don't absolutely have to. Both of you are domestics who would just as soon cook in than be taken out to the most elegant of restaurants. You share the same dewy-eyed sentimentality, shower each other with tender love tidings and emotionally empathize in those moody moments that seem like they're never going to subside.

This is a relationship of deep understanding, a high degree of compatibility and a plethora of physical passion. Because of the intense rapport and the feelings of selfless caring, it could last a lifetime.

Cancer Woman

Cancer woman with Aries man

She'll fall in love with his dynamic enthusiasm, but may get hurt by his lack of emotional understanding. She needs more nurturing than he knows how to give, and has more insecurities than he knows how to handle. He'll blunder his way through her life, and she'll hold back the tears when she sees him leaving (even for five minutes). He can't understand why she's so emotional and sometimes he feels closed off and closed in.

She's one woman who will stick by him for better or for worse. However, whether he'll stick by her is quite another story.

Cancer woman with Taurus man

You are two stay-at-home creatures and can have a lovely evening just preparing a pot of stew. At times she will remind him of mother at Christmas. He will remind her of daddy on the days that he paid the rent. In each other they find their secure fantasies satisfied, and for both that is a lot. She'll find him to be someone solid to lean on, while he will find her a cushion of kindness.

She will want to be possessed for ever and always. He wants someone to treat him like his savings account. Deep down inside, he dreams of a 'little woman' and even is she were president of a multinational corporation, she would still be willing to take on the traditional role. These two were made for each other and could spend a lifetime loving. All that they have to do is meet.

Cancer woman with Gemini man

She's a home person, but he can't be in enough places at once. She is shy, deeply emotional and very moody; he is detached, mentally, and very changeable. These two are a gnawing enigma to each other in the best moments, and a murderous annoyance in the worst. She craves emotional security, but he lives for his freedom. She needs to be made to feel secure, while he needs to be challenged.

Emotionally, this is about the least compatible combination. However, for this very reason they could be very good for each other if they are both willing to try. He could realize that he really has feelings underneath his overworked mind, and she might realize that she really has a sense of humour underneath all of those obsessive feelings and insecurities.

Cancer woman with Leo man

It might seem to him that she wants his plasma on a silver platter. She does. When it comes to love, she is a conspicuous consumer. She craves Mr Leo's total love, attention, affection, fantasies, thoughts and dreams; in other words, she wants it all. When she doesn't get her way, she gets weepy. At first this is effective, but after a few of the same performances, her repertoire reeks of repetition, and this man begins to cool off.

Her dependence will flatter him, but her demands will make him feel claustrophobic. On the first coffee date she'll enquire where she stands in the future. If he manages to get a second date, she'll ask him if he prefers a wedding in June or December.

At moments she'll be his mother; at other times, his little girl. It's very hard for her just to be a lover, because she never feels that much at ease with her own emotions.

His challenge is treating her like a woman, and letting her believe it. But that takes a very selfless kind of loving – no comment on whether Mr Leo can do it.

Cancer woman with Virgo man

Although her moods often confuse him, her intense emotions provide the encouragement that gives him tremendous comfort. He is as insecure as she is, though he covers it up with his will and his acute sense of logic. She will evoke his most vulnerable emotions, and he will help her to filter life through her head as well as her heart. However, at times he won't be as cuddly as her affectionate nature would like. He spends most of his time working, and when he's not working he's worrying about whether he could have done a better job.

He is an exceedingly analytical individual, whereas she is exceedingly emotional. But both of them can respect the other's perspective, and can learn to work through them rather than around them. This could be a relationship of lasting value that results in a sound marriage.

Cancer woman with Libra man

Not only will she give him all the little mothering attentions, she'll throw in a few more. However, after she has poured out to him endlessly, and all he has to say to her is that he can't decide what he wants in a woman, it should be a hasty goodbye. Unfortunately she'll hang around for a few more of these tender emotional scenes.

Mr Libra considers himself to be a person with feelings. He is, but they're all about himself. When he kisses her he wants to hear a love song, but all he hears is her whistling kettle. She needs to remind him that the tea is for him. It takes a lot for her to realize that it really is over, and it takes even more for Mr Libra to realize that it's even begun. The emotional timing here is so bad that it would probably take more than a lifetime for them to get together. It might be helpful if you both die and get reborn into another sign.

Cancer woman with Scorpio man

She'll nurture his needs, make him fat and happy on her cooking, and try to be understanding when he's being surly. She is kind, giving, compassionate, sympathetic and more caring than a Red Cross nurse. She'll listen to his problems, pay him more attention than he desires (or deserves!) and make him feel like he's the 'greatest show on earth'. All she wants in return is love. But she wants to be smothered in it.

He appreciates her love and affection, but something deep within him makes it difficult for him to totally accept it. He needs to keep his own space – not necessarily because he wants it, but because he has a fear that if any woman gets too close and starts to need him, she just might be taken away.

This could be a great match, just as long as he is ready to settle for some connubial bliss. Should Mr Scorpio have only a good fling in mind, then after she tells him her Sun sign she should just keep on walking.

Cancer woman with Sagittarius man

He'll see her as a drag on his independence, and she'll see him as a threat to her tentative sense of security. She'll be hurt and hostile when he doesn't even finish his dessert because he has a twilight tennis game. His patience will be provoked when she would rather sit by the fireside than go skiing.

She seeks a quiet kind of romance with someone who will provide an array of creature comforts. He seeks a short-lived affair that is more like an animal chase. His charm will probably rip right into her soul like a grenade going off in a sleepy village. Any way you look at it, these two are about as compatible as pickles and ice cream.

Cancer woman with Capricorn man

He is the security she has always longed for, while she is the woman who can give him the warmth he so needs. Between them there is an undeniable attraction and a very basic understanding.

Together they can live a cosy existence, showering lots of love on each other and sharing many intense moments. Within the depths of their feelings he will be able to see the same insecurities that bring on his own melancholic moments. The more they allow their sensitivity to expand into the depths of each other, the more emotionally rich their lives will ultimately be. And, once they've had it, they can't deny that this is the greatest kind of wealth.

Cancer woman with Aquarius man

She lives by her emotions, whereas he relies on his logic. This creates a kind of friction that may be more than either of them can stand. She may think she has to knock him out with a swift karate chop and then hypnotize him with the right words just to get a little romance going.

When she makes him a pie, he'll take it apart, stare at it for a while, ask what's in it, then forget to eat it because he's too busy talking. Needless to say, Mr Aquarius gets more pleasure in finding out how the whole thing works than he does in the actual experience.

Although he is a good, hearty sort, he sometimes gets so entangled in his theories that he reminds her of a mad scientist who sleeps with test tubes under his pillow. If she wants a man who will hug her, make mad, passionate love and remind her how much she means to him, she'd better start looking elsewhere.

Cancer woman with Pisces man

He will find her nice to cuddle. She will create a plethora of seductive creature comforts and provide the emotional backup he needs to do his best. Not only is she warm and sensitive, she also has the kind of womanly strength that reminds him of his mother. She will understand his moods, listen to his problems and lend him a lot of loving assistance for those projects he knows he'll never finish.

In essence, this combination could be a divine exploration into the deepest experience of love. Communication here may carry her out to the farthest planes of feeling.

Cancer Man

Cancer man with Aries woman

He is a truly lovable person, but his love is not meant for her. Her fiery outbursts will send him into sullen withdrawal, and his sullen withdrawals will send her through more fiery outbursts. The two of them are so different that it's as if they come from two distinct foreign countries, neither of which knew the other even existed.

Emotionally she is super-sensitive, though hates to show it. She has a way of hurting his feelings even by the way she asks him a polite question. Her feeble attempts to camouflage her vulnerability make her chew her nails. His moods make her more than impatient, and his apparent placidity makes her stamp her feet just to break the silence. If Ms Aries wants a lot of drama, she'd be better off going to a movie, or finding someone else.

Cancer man with Taurus woman

A great deal of passion will pass between these two, but whether the relationship endures will depend on whether they are both willing to take it.

He is loyal and loving, but the meaning of his moods will totally elude her. One moment he is insecure and dependent, the next he is totally withdrawn. Her feelings have a way of

tying them both up in knots. However, together they will sati-
ate each other's security needs. She is the earthy foundation
to his ivory tower made of molten wax.

She tends to dwell on fundamentals, while he lingers on
the romantic overtones. He is carried away by softness and
subtlety; she is more entranced by some support. Both are so
jealous that they make each other feel sought-after when they
trade suspicions. And both are so domestic that together they
can spend a weekend cooking up a storm.

In most respects this relationship is highly compatible,
because when you combine earth with water the result is fer-
tility and sustained emotion.

Cancer man with Gemini woman

He is emotional and vulnerable, while outwardly she is cool
and controlled. He is often victimized by his feelings; she is
put out of control by her mind.

This is one relationship where communication is definitely
going in different directions. He is so super-sensitive that he
considers her friendliness to other people purposefully insult-
ing. And when he sulks over his steak and refuses to tell her
the time, she comes to the conclusion that he would be better
off with a waitress.

They both have a way of bringing out the other's most
painful insecurities; it's a kind of emotional immolation. She
has a way of laughing at times when he wants her to be serious, and he has a way of being glacial when she needs some
warmth. Their only real hope is to stop chatting and start talking. Decide to be brave, put away emotional masks and sup-
ports and try leaning on each other.

♋

Cancer man with Leo woman

Although he loves romantic games, he is soon defiled by the reality of her emotions. He has probably called her 12 times a day for countless days, and she's always busy. On the first call he is extremely interested, by the sixth he is morosely impassioned, and by the ninth he has feverishly abandoned all control.

For even her Leo sensibilities, his histrionics are indecently excessive; at his most dramatic he is dark and brooding. When his senses are unappeased, he melts into melancholia and defiant doldrums. He tries to get her attention by not speaking or calling, and with relief Ms Leo surmises that he's finally found some self-respect. With discipline, he can prolong his confinement because he wants to make her suffer even more from his silence. When he decides that he can no longer stand it, his clammy fingers find their way to the telephone. Assuming a cold, aloof manner he invites her to the south of France for the weekend. And she tells him she has to wash her hair. Gulping with great dignity, he invites her to midnight dancing, Sunday lunch and the late-afternoon double feature, seven weeks from next Saturday. Graciously, she explains that she will be cleaning her cupboards. What he doesn't realize is that even if Ms Leo's love life were non-existent, she could never persuade herself into considering him.

Cancer man with Virgo woman

He'll make her feel like a 19th-century *femme fatale* in a picture hat. He'll heartily respond to her shyness, her little insecurities, her warmth and the way her face flushes when he compliments her. She'll love the way he courts her. She'll treasure his concern when she has a slight cold, and she'll be thankful for the way his affection makes her feel finally appreciated.

For one of the first times in her life, she feels secure in her feelings, while he feels that this is a fantasy he's always hoped for. Together, they can take each other to many wondrous emotional places, and enjoy the kind of emotional happiness they've never known before.

Cancer man with Libra woman

He'll give her all the attention she so craves, and will delight in creating those cosy stay-at-home evenings she loves. At dinner parties he'll help her cook and will probably originate a few gastronomical delights of his own. However, he will question why she has to spend huge amounts of money on saucepans and only slightly less on new boots when last year's still look perfectly new – to him, anyway. There will be moments when his moodiness will make her morose. But none of this will diminish the joy they can experience together.

He's sensitive, kind and caring, even if he has to cut off his emotions in an effort to discover her vulnerability; Ms Libra will help him restore his emotional balance. He wants a woman he can be secure with and she wants the same from a man, plus the pleasures of shared experience. Together they could create a romance of which only dreams are made. And with all of his charms, it's an easy task to transform a dream into the most romantic kind of reality.

Cancer man with Scorpio woman

For her, he's a package deal – a man with the qualities of a mother. He'll understand her moods, kiss her on the temples, bake her apple pies and serve her tea with lemon. This combination is highly compatible, especially if she was born in the last 10 days of the Scorpio period.

As long as she respects his feelings, he'll be kind and

caring, and happy to be controlled by her feminine power. Once she makes him feel secure, he will be loyal, proud and possessive. He'll romance her personality and give her total power. He'll let her take him wherever she wants to go, and make it known that she is the journey that he has always wanted to take.

Cancer man with Sagittarius woman

He needs her beside him, but she needs the space to be by herself. She'll undoubtedly inflict a mortal wound when she asks why he's so dependent. But she'll bring him to the verge of suicide when he hands her a love poem and she laughs and shrieks, 'You've got to be kidding!'

She'll never understand his sensitivities, and he'll never understand her need for freedom. He'll become so infatuated with her vitality and sense of humour that he'll want to follow her even to the supermarket and spend time with her while she stands in the queue. He'll get emotional over the way she butters her scones, and when she's not looking he'll fondle her tennis racket. Much of the time he's with her he'll spend sulking in conspicuous silence, feverishly hoping that she's eating her heart out. However, she cheerfully slaps him on the back and asks if he has indigestion. All hope is lost, and he suddenly decides he wants to go home.

Cancer man with Capricorn woman

She'll be touched by the way he cares for her welfare, but will have a hard time dealing with his moods.

He seems to create slights and then sulk about them. No matter how hard she tries, she can never discover what she's done wrong. He'll resent all the time she spends at the office, not to mention cocktail parties that seem to enhance business.

In turn, she'll resent his suspicions and the way he makes her feel guilty when she tries to ignore him. If she can manage to look at him from a less superficial standpoint, she may find the man who is very much worthy of her attentions. However, she'll have to pay in kind for his sympathy and services.

Cancer man with Aquarius woman

He creates closeness, but she feels more comfortable at a distance. He prefers cosy tête-à-têtes, while she embraces crowded scenes. He enjoys quiet evenings at home, while she prefers mass riots. The difference between these two can be awesome: he needs a woman who will nurture his strength and overlook his insecurities; she needs a man who has fewer insecurities and a greater degree of emotional detachment.

Since she's adaptable to most personalities, she could come to love his. However, if he drowns her in a swamp of emotions and makes too many demands, she'll leave him to his sentimental dreams and memories of an affair that might have been.

Cancer man with Pisces woman

This psychic rapport will leave him starry-eyed. He will sympathize with her mood swings, cry along with her during a teary old movie and remember what she wore on the day he first met her. She'll marvel that he is a better cook than she is, is equally as sensitive and seems to know not only what she's thinking, but why.

They'll both find themselves saying the same things simultaneously; they'll finish each other's sentences and respect each other's ideas. This relationship is one made for lazy summer weekends by the sea, and champagne and candlelight evenings.

Your Child of the Zodiac

As the parents of a Cancerian child you soon get used to his or her surprising and sometimes infuriating mood swings. This sensitive little soul can be laughing one minute and sobbing his/her heart out the next. Moon children are intuitive and have their own personal radar system always ready to detect any anger or sadness in the atmosphere. This sometimes means that he or she gets upset about something that hasn't even happened. This child has an extraordinary and colourful imagination and can sometimes be subject to nightmares or worries about the future. Encouraging him or her to talk about any fears is the quickest way to help overcome them. Worry and stress may be responsible for many of the minor stomach upsets that are sometimes a feature of Cancerian childhood.

The Cancerian child can seem to be obedient and docile, but you may have found out the hard way that he or she has a will of iron. Crabs learn early on what is theirs, and you may often find yourself trying to get them to share their toys with their friends. The young Cancerian can be easily hurt and you may have to explain that it is sometimes necessary to forgive and forget. Despite normally being an easy-going and friendly child, a young Crab is never frightened to stand up for him- or herself. This child is especially upset if his or her peers are careless with toys and books. Don't worry if your little Crab seems to be a bit short of playmates. Quality, not quantity, is important. You will find that as your child grows older, he or she will probably maintain the select circle of friends that was established early on.

Your Cancerian child will enjoy school once the initial strangeness has worn off. Young Crabs are not usually disruptive in the classroom but can sometimes get over-excited, leading to mischievous spells. Learning will most likely come easily and any opportunity to express his or her creativity should be encouraged. Your child probably enjoys dressing up and painting, and could even turn these kinds of activities into a career. Boy or girl, your child will enjoy cooking. Time spent learning how to prepare simple meals with mum or dad is a perfect example of quality time. Gardening is another pastime that the family can share. You may be surprised at how absorbed your Cancerian child becomes when given his or her own little patch of land to cultivate.

Crab children are extremely affectionate. Sometimes your child may be a bit clingy, but that usually only happens if he or she is unwell or feels insecure. Your child's ability to nurture others shows in relationships with younger brothers or sisters. Young Cancerians are sometimes old for their years and think nothing of helping out if you are too busy. If your child has no siblings, a pet could be a much-loved addition to the family.

However, your Cancerian child is probably most content when enjoying your undivided attention. You must have noticed how much he or she looks forward to a bedtime story or a quiet period after school when you listen to all the day's exploits. Feeling really secure at home gives your Cancerian child the confidence to explore the wider world. But always remember that if there should be bad news or you have something disappointing or difficult to say, hiding it from your child is the worst possible option. A Cancerian child always knows when there is something wrong and, by hiding the truth, you are in actual fact giving your child far more opportunity to worry than if you keep him or her in the picture in the first place. These are special children, blessed with the ability to know when others need cheering up, and with the warmth and humour to be able to do so.

Monthly and Daily Guides

JANUARY

This Sun is digging its way through earthy Capricorn, as usual at this time of year. This is your opposite number and you and your partner will have plenty to talk about, perhaps making plans for the year to come. On 20 January the Sun enters airy Aquarius, and you and your partner will still be discussing future plans but this time it will be linked to your finances. If you are thinking of moving house, you might be doing the sums to see what you can afford.

There is a Sagittarian influence to the New Year, putting the emphasis on your daily routine and health matters. Mercury begins the month in Sagittarius and one of your New Year's resolutions could be to streamline all your chores so that you have more time for things you enjoy doing. On 10 January, Mercury drifts into Capricorn and you'll probably have friends ringing up from all over the world who might have missed you at Christmas. At the end the month, on 30 January, Mercury moves into Aquarius.

Venus also starts the year in Sagittarius, and as this is the over-indulgence section in your chart, you may be scoffing the last of those festive chocolates and left over titbits. On 10 January Venus enters Capricorn, ensuring that whatever discussions you have with your partner, you seem to be in agreement. If you're on your own, there will be plenty of invitations that you just can't refuse.

Mars is placed in fiery Sagittarius for the entire month, which will mean that you're very busy but you will at least have all the energy you require to get through even the dreariest of tasks. If you have put on a few pounds over the holiday season, this is an ideal placement under which to start a fitness regime, even though this may not really be your style!

The planets are emphasizing close relationships this month and, in keeping with tradition, it really is time to plan ahead.

1 SATURDAY

New Year's Day really is one for relaxing, don't you agree? With the Sun in your opposite number, you may enjoy just sitting around with your loved ones or chatting on the phone to friends and relatives. However, at the back of your mind there is a nagging feeling that perhaps you should be doing something constructive.

2 SUNDAY

Giving yourself a hard time about how much there is to do is not really very practical. You have fantastic intuition and instincts and if you give yourself a moment to mentally prioritize all your jobs, you may find that there isn't quite as much hanging over your head as you thought.

3 MONDAY

It's possible that today is still a holiday from work for you
and, in fact, home is exactly where you want to be. It may be a
cliché that you are a home-loving sign but that doesn't mean
it isn't true, and perhaps you are looking at your surroundings now and wondering how you can improve them. Let
your imagination take over.

4 TUESDAY

Just when you thought the festivities were all over, some visitors arrive. Knowing you, your fridge is still stuffed with
goodies, and I'm sure there is plenty of booze left over to toast
the New Year. In fact there's nothing you like better than
entertaining at home, so relax and enjoy yourself.

5 WEDNESDAY

If you're a parent, your children could be a bit of a handful at
the moment. After a while, it becomes a headache to keep
them entertained, don't you think? Why not set them a few
little tasks to do around the house to keep them occupied, and
also to help you out?

6 THURSDAY

Socializing could be expensive, so you really need to set yourself a budget if you're out and about this evening. Of course,
it doesn't mean it isn't going to be fun, and if you're single
you could meet someone rather attractive. Don't take this
seriously but view it as a sign that this year you really are
going to have a good time.

7 FRIDAY

Perhaps you're a bit tired and, if so, you might be a little snappy today. If you're not careful you are going to say exactly the wrong thing to the wrong person. Do try and think before you react, as you could be giving a very bad impression of yourself otherwise.

8 SATURDAY

The concentration of planets in the routine and health section of your chart is urging you to spring-clean your body and mind. There is no question that you love your food, and you may even be a bit of a gourmet cook on the quiet, but I think it might be time to put away those delicious French recipe books and concentrate on a bit of careful detoxing!

9 SUNDAY

Venus is getting ready to move into earthy Capricorn now, throwing a rosy glow over your closest relationship. However, you may find that you and your partner have important matters to discuss and it is possible that you're coming at the problem from two completely different directions. Compromise is essential if you're to make the most of the next few weeks.

10 MONDAY

There is a New Moon in Capricorn today, which, as you know, is your opposite number. New Moons indicate the opportunity for a new beginning. If you and a colleague have been at odds recently it could reach a climax today. You now have the chance to put this relationship onto a fresh footing.

11 TUESDAY

Yesterday Mercury moved into Capricorn where it joined the
Sun and Venus. You may be surprised at how simple it was to
make the first move towards reconciliation. Your fear of rejection sometimes prevents you from extending the hand of
friendship. It appears that you are turning over a new leaf this
year, perhaps learning how to make the first move?

12 WEDNESDAY

If you're footloose and fancy-free and a friend suggests that
you join forces and holiday together, don't think twice. It's
always a good idea to have something positive to look forward to, and sometimes you can dwell too much in the past,
can't you?

13 THURSDAY

Now that you've got the travel bug, there's no stopping you,
is there? In fact you come up with some bright ideas of your
own, and as far as you're concerned the further away and the
more exotic the better. This change in your outlook surprises
those who know you best, which is no bad thing.

14 FRIDAY

If you've got itchy feet at work, something that happens
today may make you decide it really is time to move on.
You're not often impulsive and the chances of you storming
out in a huff are almost nil. However, once you make a decision you do tend to stick to it, and you will be putting all your
energies into finding something that suits you better.

15 SATURDAY

This is not a lazy day, as you scour the situations vacant columns in all the newspapers. When you have an idea in your head nothing and no one is going to push it aside. In fact, you may become a bit of a bore about your career prospects, so keep some of your more tedious thoughts to yourself.

16 SUNDAY

A professional concern may still be dominating the conversation and people you live with, whether they are family or flat-mates, could be getting a little bit tired of it. As far as they're concerned, whatever would make you happy is fine by them, but none of them can make the decision for you, can they?

17 MONDAY

The people you meet today, whether they are old friends or complete strangers, could have a far-reaching effect on your life. Sometimes you are resistant to new ideas but the planets are urging you to be more open to outside influences. Because you're so sensitive, sometimes you feel the need to protect yourself, but at the moment only positive influences are coming your way.

18 TUESDAY

If you're part of a team at work, then today's efforts are going to bring wonderful results. Usually you prefer to be a foot soldier in the background, but today you seem to be in charge of the troops. Surprisingly, you actually find you enjoy this.

19 WEDNESDAY

It's tempting to withdraw into your shell as you know better than most that a degree of solitude is useful to mull over future plans and projects. However, the planets are still encouraging you to socialize and mix with people from different backgrounds. You can always leave an important social event early, can't you?

20 THURSDAY

The Sun moves into airy and eccentric Aquarius and the spotlight turns to financial assets and responsibilities you share with someone else. Perhaps you and your partner have been discussing a major purchase, or possibly even a change of residence, and now you are spurred on to get down to the details.

21 FRIDAY

Your sensitivity can sometimes lead you astray. You may be under the impression that a friend or colleague is working against you. Is it possible you've got the wrong end of the stick? Confrontation is not your style, but a degree of frostiness is, which in turn invites a cold response. Be careful you're not barking up the wrong tree.

22 SATURDAY

The Moon will be in Cancer for the next couple of days which as its your ruling planet, heightens your intuition. But remember: instincts are only helpful if they are correct and free from preconceived ideas. If you have an erroneous idea about a friend or colleague, you're likely to make a costly mistake.

23 SUNDAY

Oh dear! You run the risk of really spoiling what could be a lovely day. Whatever is the matter with you? Sometimes your sensitivity drifts towards paranoia and your inability to be straightforward can drive friends and loved ones to distraction.

24 MONDAY

You may feel like shutting up shop and keeping yourself to yourself but that will only succeed in making you feel even more isolated. I know it's very hard for you to reach out to others when you are feeling insecure, but this is exactly what you must do today or you'll end up being even more miserable.

25 TUESDAY

There is a Full Moon in Leo today and if you have any sense at all you will decide to smile and forget all about recent upsets. If you really can't change tack just yet, perhaps you need to indulge in some retail therapy.

26 WEDNESDAY

Your boss may present you with an onerous task that you really would rather do without. Resist the temptation to feel picked on, because in actual fact this is a reward. If that doesn't make sense to you, try looking at it from a different perspective. He or she obviously thinks you are well up to the job.

27 THURSDAY

Your family are very important to you and if you haven't seen your brothers and sisters recently, you'll be longing to get together with them now. In fact, no sooner have you thought of them than one of them is on the phone trying to organize a meeting. I'm sure this cheers you up no end.

28 FRIDAY

It may not just be a social occasion that a brother or sister has in mind. He or she may have something serious to talk about and needs your opinion and insight. You are more than ready to come up with one or two ideas that will help.

29 SATURDAY

There seem to be a lot of little jobs that need your attention this weekend and, while you may be longing to be somewhere else, they keep you rooted close to home. It's funny isn't it? Usually there is nothing you like better than pottering around at home, but right at this moment you would much rather be somewhere else.

30 SUNDAY

Mercury moves into airy Aquarius and future plans involving large sums of money become the focus of your attention. Try not to get too carried away in the immediate future as you could be pursuing an ideal that isn't really in your best interests.

31 MONDAY

Now you are back at work, you are hankering after your home! Are you just being contrary? I don't think so. It's just that you feel a little bit unsettled and you're so governed by your moods that sometimes you get everything out of proportion. You may not have much time to think about changes you'd like to make on the home front during the day but this evening there is nothing to stop you planning and scheming, is there?

FEBRUARY

Well the Sun is breezing through Aquarius and you and your partner could be making expensive plans for the future. Don't make any concrete commitments until later on in the month or you could find that you lose out financially. On 19 February the Sun drifts into Pisces, a water sign like your good self. This is an inspirational position and you can really feel the dark days of winter are beginning to recede and spring is on its way.

Mercury continues in Aquarius for a couple of weeks, and while you are concentrating on facts and figures you may become a little bit single minded. Try and give yourself a bit of space to dream. On the 17th Mercury enters Pisces, and you are sure to be mixing with some interesting people, possibly from abroad. This is bound to stimulate your sense of adventure.

On 3 February Venus enters Aquarius, the section of your chart that not only rules joint financial responsibilities but also sharing on a more intimate basis. A new relationship could move on to a different level, if you want it to. Venus also moves into Pisces this month, but not until the 26th, and I'll discuss this in more detail next month.

Mars will still be situated in Sagittarius for a few days, then moves into your opposite number, Capricorn, on 7 February. Mars provides us with energy and enthusiasm but also the potential to be antagonistic simply for the sake of it. If you find yourself on the receiving end of other people's anger, it's important that you examine your own behaviour to see if you could be contributing to this.

There is a change in Jupiter's direction on 2 February. Jolly Jupiter is currently situated in Libra, right at the bottom of your chart, in the section linked to your home life and most intimate thoughts. However, from now on it will be retrograde for a few months, and changes that you want put into place at home may have to be put on hold for the time being. Don't be too disappointed about this as it gives you an opportunity to refine your plans and make sure that they are absolutely spot on.

1 TUESDAY

You could be very tempted by an expensive item you see, or possibly, if you're house hunting, what looks like your dream home. You really do need to consider your options very carefully before you make any move. Planetary positionings over the next couple of weeks indicate that you could be missing something crucial, so do be patient, won't you?

2 WEDNESDAY

Jupiter changes direction today and, for reasons best known to itself, it will be moving in retrograde motion for the next few months. As it is now in Libra and in the section of your chart linked to your domestic life, you could become a little frustrated or impatient if your home is not the peaceful haven you need it to be. Don't make any rash decisions if possible.

3 THURSDAY

Venus breezes into airy Aquarius and some of you may be beginning to suspect that a casual friendship could have a bit more going for it than you first thought. As you are unlikely to make the first move, this could take a while to get going. Of course you can always drop a few hints, can't you?

4 FRIDAY

If you wake up this morning feeling a bit down in the dumps, you need to give yourself a good talking to. OK, so things are not going to proceed at the speed that you had hoped, but sometimes life has a way of giving us what we need instead of what we think we want. Retain your vision and take a new approach to the details.

5 SATURDAY

If you have a mountain of domestic chores to get through today, you could be forgiven for feeling a little bit hard done by. You can be a perfectionist when it comes to your surroundings but sometimes all you do is give yourself extra work. Give yourself a deadline and refuse point-blank to do anything dreary after that time.

6 SUNDAY

Mars is on the move into your opposite number Capricorn and you must be careful not to antagonize friends, loved ones and even, I'm afraid to say, complete strangers. Pent-up frustration and anger find a release somewhere and if you're not in touch with your feelings, some outsider may use you as a scapegoat for their own.

7 MONDAY

If you're in a long-term and serious relationship, your partner may be in a mood that you just can't fathom out. Perhaps your frustration at work has meant you aren't very good company at home. While your partner is happy to support you, he or she doesn't want to hear every detail of your professional grievances.

8 TUESDAY

Well, there is a New Moon in Aquarius today and you have an opportunity to examine exactly where you stand financially. Something may come to light that you hadn't thought of, and if it is linked to a major purchase, such as a mortgage, you'll be very glad that you are in possession of this information.

9 WEDNESDAY

It's time to get your thinking cap on and if you and your partner, or anyone else that you share financial responsibilities or assets with, get together, you can come up with a solution that suits everybody. It's important, however, that you still put off signing any important paperwork until after you have checked every detail.

10 THURSDAY

At heart you're an imaginative soul, and too much concentration on facts and figures gets you down in the end. Of course, if it's in your own interests you will persevere, but you would much rather be creating mind pictures of your future. Sometimes it's useful to take a step back from day-to-day reality, don't you agree?

11 FRIDAY

Thinking outside the box is the way that entrepreneurs make their fortunes. Perhaps you're not quite in this position today but you do seem to have an unorthodox way of looking at things. Rather than keeping this to yourself, letting your colleagues in on your secret will help everyone, and you'll be the one getting all the praise.

12 SATURDAY

You may be tempted to blow your own trumpet today, although this doesn't really come naturally. In some ways, attracting attention feels a little bit intrusive, but you really do want to let your circle know about your recent little triumphs. And why not?

13 SUNDAY

Your little grey cells are all on red alert today and family and friends are not going to be able to keep up with you. Of course, as far as you're concerned, unless you have the people you love supporting you, it doesn't matter how many opportunities you're offered, you aren't going to take them. Now, however, it's time to make one decision purely and simply for yourself.

14 MONDAY

Romantics like yourself couldn't forget what day it is today. If your partner is the sort of person that regards Valentine's Day as a cheap con-trick, you may find yourself a little bit disappointed. I'm sure when he or she sees how crestfallen you are, every effort possible will be made to cheer you up.

15 TUESDAY

Eating out with friends may help you see a relationship in a more realistic perspective. If you're hooked up with someone who doesn't really pay much attention to anniversaries but is there for you in every other respect, you need to count your blessings!

16 WEDNESDAY

You could find yourself drifting off into fantasy land from time to time today. This is OK if no one is depending on you for anything at all. If they are, whether it's colleagues or your family, you may get short shrift and end up feeling guilty that you haven't come up with the goods.

17 THURSDAY

Mercury trips into Pisces today and all of a sudden you feel a weight has been lifted from your shoulders. You can be enthusiastic now about future projects, especially if you're planning to do some travelling in the near future. In fact, you may even receive some news from abroad that confirms you are on the right path.

18 FRIDAY

There could be a surprise meeting of minds today – literally! Perhaps you bump into someone you've lost touch with and he or she is full of bright ideas and has plenty of news that cheers you up. You're susceptible to other people's moods and you need to surround yourself with positive influences.

19 SATURDAY

The Sun joins Mercury in watery Pisces and you may find it even more difficult to concentrate on routine chores. But really, if you don't get them done they are just going to pile up until it is a mountain that you really can't climb. Put your dreams on the back-burner for a bit and focus on the job in hand.

20 SUNDAY

It is in your nature to be changeable, and you yourself don't always understand why one minute you are filled with joy

and the next feeling down the dumps. Serious issues may
have clouded your mind from time to time over the last year
or so and some of you may realize that one relationship has
just got to change or die. As you hate letting go of anything,
this is causing you a good deal of pain.

21 MONDAY

Inspiration can strike at any time, anywhere. You could be on
the bus, at work or even in the bath, which I'm sure is one of
your favourite places! Suddenly you realize that certain pre-
conceptions you have been clinging on to are of absolutely no
use whatsoever. It's true that we create our own reality, and
we can also change it whenever we choose to, don't you
agree?

22 TUESDAY

Be careful if you are shopping, as deceptive influences indicate you could be short changed or buy something that falls
apart the minute you get it home. In fact, if in doubt, don't!
It's also worth checking all your domestic paperwork, just to
make sure you haven't overlooked an important bill or bank
statement.

23 WEDNESDAY

You may be focusing on much more romantic and intriguing
prospects but you have decided it's time to have a big clear-
up at home. While you love your home, it doesn't necessarily
mean that you are traditionally house proud and, in fact, the
more clutter there is around you, the more secure you tend to
feel. But sometimes you need to clear a path through all the
confusion, don't you?

24 THURSDAY
There is a Full Moon today in picky and fastidious Virgo. This
rules the section of your chart linked to your local neighbourhood and there may have been one or two little local errands
or meetings that have been outstanding for a while. Suddenly
it seems imperative that you get them done, but if you're in
too much of a hurry, you may have to retrace your steps at a
later date.

25 FRIDAY
You rarely argue simply for the sake of it, but someone may
drive you into a rage today. Perhaps you are just feeling a bit
at odds with the world, or maybe a little bit tired, but if you're
driving you need to be really, really careful or you could find
yourself dealing with a minor prang or dispute.

26 SATURDAY
Venus drifts into watery Pisces and, if you're single, you
could find yourself being attracted to someone very different
from your usual type. Sometimes, because you cling to the
past, you tend to mix with people that have a similar outlook.
But these days you're changing, aren't you? You have nothing
to lose by getting to know him or her a bit better.

27 SUNDAY
No one can make a meal as comforting, relaxing and delicious
as you. Perhaps you have invited friends or family round for
Sunday lunch; it has the potential to be a delightful opportunity for good conversation and great food. You are in your
element when you are surrounded by the ones you love and
who appreciate your generosity.

28 MONDAY

Perhaps you've got a bit of a sore head today but it was all worthwhile, nevertheless. If you're a little bit grumpy with colleagues or people you see on a regular basis, you may not even realize it. Possibly a hot bath and an early night are in order this evening, don't you agree?

MARCH

If you are typical Crab, close relationships are of the utmost importance to you, and as Saturn has been grinding its way through your sign for the best part of two years, you may have seen some major changes in your closest partnerships. Some of you may have found yourself single again after a long time, and some of you may wish you were! It's likely that the majority of you have found out exactly how much you appreciate your other half. On 22 March, Saturn turns direct and begins the final stages of its journey through Cancer. If you have been puzzled by emotional upsets over the last couple of years, you will now know exactly why things happened the way that they did. The only way now is up!

Pluto, currently in Sagittarius, also changes direction this month, turning retrograde on 27 March. If you are hoping to make changes in your job, you may have to put them on hold. But don't let go of your dreams: this is simply an opportunity to refine your plans.

What about the regular planetary movements? The Sun continues in Pisces during most of March, allowing your imagination to soar and any contact you have with people living overseas to flourish. On the 21st the Sun enters Aries and career matters will definitely be on the agenda.

Remember not to get too disheartened if you find a promising road only leads to a dead end.

Mercury spends a few days in Pisces and on 5 March it too enters Aries. This is usually a helpful position for you, especially if you're ambitious, but unfortunately Mercury turns retrograde on 20 March and it's a wise Crab that resists signing contracts or making too many unnecessary journeys at this time, particularly in connection with work.

Venus continues in Pisces for a while, reinforcing pleasant connections with foreigners. Should you be involved in any legal proceedings, Venus will be very helpful at this time, especially if you're waiting for financial compensation. On 23 March Venus moves into Aries and you find yourself mixing business with pleasure. In fact if you are hoping to make progress in your career, the more people you charm, the better it will be for your prospects, even if nothing happens immediately.

Mars is still in Capricorn, your opposite number, so do be diplomatic at all times. Of course you may be boiling over with rage under the surface, but try not to let it show. On 21 March Mars moves into Aquarius and finances and big business benefit from its assertive and courageous energy. If you're involved in any financial wheeling and dealing you can take a risk, so long as you do it this month rather than the next.

1 TUESDAY

The watery feel to the planets today ensures that you start the month off in a good mood. Of course, you may have the usual niggles worrying you, but some days you just feel that the good really does outweigh the bad, don't you? In fact you may come up with the perfect solution to one outstanding dilemma without even trying today.

2 WEDNESDAY

Your mood continues to be buoyant, and if you've had a few schemes bubbling away on the back-burner it might be an idea to take one out and have a look at it. Bear in mind that the go-ahead for it is still a little way away, but it doesn't hurt to tinker with something in the meantime, does it?

3 THURSDAY

If you get the urge to look through some old photo albums or sort out all those piles of letters you've kept since you were a child, you may find something of interest. Perhaps you are reminded of someone you've lost touch with and decide you are going to make an effort to contact him or her.

4 FRIDAY

You may feel as though you've been pushing yourself a little bit too hard lately but it does seem as though the pressure is going to continue, at least for today. Promise yourself a reward this weekend and it won't seem quite such hard going. In fact, you may get a second wind and breeze through the afternoon's chores.

5 SATURDAY

Mercury moves into Aries and the zenith point of your chart. While this position is primarily concerned with your career, it also puts you in the public eye. Of course, we are not all film stars, but it might mean that your phone rings continually today with people who've suddenly decided they need to speak to you or see you, right now!

6 SUNDAY

Sometimes you can be your own worst enemy, especially when you're being stubborn. That hard outer shell sometimes prevents you from seeing what are your own best interests. If your partner has suggested something that isn't immediately attractive, it may be worth having second thoughts. After all, getting your own way all the time isn't good for you, I think you'll agree.

7 MONDAY

Perhaps your conscience is troubling you, especially if you feel you were a bit mean to your partner. Why don't you ring your lover up to say how much you love him or her? I'm sure the response will be delightful and you can make up for lost time this evening.

8 TUESDAY

You may have a hunch today which could be worth backing. I'm not suggesting you spend all your wages betting on the horses, but if you feel the need to contact someone who could be helpful to you, you may well be right. After all, it doesn't hurt to raise your profile a little bit.

9 WEDNESDAY

Your intuition is really spot on the moment, probably because the Moon is now in Pisces, making you feel emotionally secure. Bright ideas are coming thick and fast, and if you can jot them down straightaway you can come back to them later and see if they make any sense.

10 THURSDAY

Today's New Moon in Pisces may bring you some welcome news from abroad. Or maybe you've confirmed your dream holiday of a lifetime for later in the year. If your life seems to have been lacking a sense of purpose lately, you may decide here and now exactly how you want to live it, and what your first step should be.

11 FRIDAY

Make sure you're looking your best today if you're at work, or just going through your regular routine. If you're a single Crab and you are looking for love, you may find yourself getting much more attention than usual. Try not to withdraw into your shell; enjoy it for a change.

12 SATURDAY

If you have a young family, you should devote all your time and energy to them today. I know this is preaching to the converted but it does seem that you have been concentrating on your career recently. Don't think it hasn't gone unnoticed at home, although your loved ones will continue to support your ambitions.

13 SUNDAY

You are in a sociable mood and even if your partner or flat-mates would prefer a quiet day, I'm sure you can manage to talk them round. If you invite a few friends around for a drink or a snack it will soon turn into a lively affair. Even the most reluctant individual can't help but join in the fun.

14 MONDAY

It's worth dragging yourself to a social event this evening, even if all you want to do is snuggle up at home. There may be a new face in your circle who is rather attractive and possibly even a little dangerous. While he or she may not be your usual type, you can't help but be intrigued.

15 TUESDAY

It seems everyone is taking their cue from you at the moment, which is rather unusual, I think you'll agree. You might prefer to keep your thoughts to yourself rather than go out on a limb, but right now you seem to be the one with the best sense of direction. Professionally this is only the beginning, as you may realize just how much you like being in charge.

16 WEDNESDAY

You've got plenty to think about in light of recent events, and you might want a few quiet nights now to mull over all the exciting new things that have been happening. Whether this involves your professional ambitions or your personal and most intimate dreams, you do need a bit of time on your own to reflect.

17 THURSDAY

Routine chores seem to be a very unwelcome interruption now, spoiling your train of thought. Unfortunately, certain responsibilities don't go away just because you feel like taking a holiday. You'll be especially aware of this if you're a parent, as the kids seem to need constant attention today. Usually this is your greatest pleasure but right now you may be longing for Mary Poppins to make an appearance.

18 FRIDAY

However hard you try to conceal your emotional nature, there are times when it's clear to all and sundry exactly what your feelings are. After all, for someone who lives mainly by following your heart it's not surprising that your friends and family always know when things aren't quite right. Of course, they rarely have any idea of the reasons for your moods, do they?

19 SATURDAY

If you find yourself pushing people away when all they want to do is help, you need to understand the reasons why. If you are feeling insecure, it may be because of a complete misunderstanding with someone close. He or she may be blissfully unaware that you are feeling rejected and the only way to explain this is directly. Not one of your natural assets, I'm afraid.

20 SUNDAY

It's a very busy few days for the planets, with the Sun and Mars both changing signs tomorrow and Mercury turning retrograde in Aries today. Remember that the periods when Mercury is retrograde indicate a time when communications can become muddled and short journeys, especially connected with work in your case, are delayed or even cancelled.

21 MONDAY

The Sun joins Mercury in Aries, and ambitious Cancerians may be feeling somewhat frustrated as your professional plans receive a setback. Try not to be too disheartened, and remember that what is for you won't pass you by. Meanwhile, Mars also moves today – in its case to airy Aquarius – so perhaps you should spend your energy focusing on important financial considerations.

22 TUESDAY

Saturn, the planet we love to hate, turns direct today, in your own sign of Cancer. This is a significant moment for you as, during the next few months, relationship issues will be of the utmost importance. Some of you may decide it's time to tie the knot, but others may realize your current partnership has very little future. Either way, a fresh start is indicated.

23 WEDNESDAY

More planetary movement today, as Venus moves into Aries. As you know, this is the zenith of your chart and you could be mixing business with pleasure. As major schemes could be on hold for a while, networking is the ideal way to spend your time, storing up Brownie points for the future.

24 THURSDAY

Your instincts may be telling you that a member of your close family needs your special brand of support. You often know when the people you love are troubled and I suggest that you make the first move and get on the phone quickly. Of course there may be nothing wrong, but it doesn't hurt to touch base, does it?

25 FRIDAY

There is a Full Moon in Libra today and there could be a few fireworks on the home front. Perhaps you and a flatmate have fallen out in connection with domestic responsibilities. Or a teenage child could be going through that awkward stage and you may be tearing your hair out at the roots.

♋

26 SATURDAY

Rather than relaxing you may feel somewhat edgy today. An intuitive and watery sign like you can feel a little at odds with the universe when most of the planets are in air and fire signs. This kind of energy jars with your sensitivity and you may find others a little too abrupt and direct for your liking.

27 SUNDAY

Pluto decides to turn retrograde today, for reasons best known to itself. On its long journey through Sagittarius, it has gradually transformed the way you work and how you organize your routines. Now that spring is here, if you've avoided it so far, you may decide it's time for a new fitness regime into the bargain.

28 MONDAY

An unexpected invitation, either to lunch or for a meal or drink after work, could make you rather excited and flattered. Of course, if you're single, this is something very welcome but if you have a partner waiting for you at home, you may need to be a little bit careful.

29 TUESDAY

There could be all sorts of mix-ups at work and it seems to be up to you to take charge. This is not something that you are accustomed to naturally, but over the last couple of months you have realized that you have more than enough skill and talent to take responsibility. Be patient if confusion still seems to be ever-present.

30 WEDNESDAY

Despite the odds being stacked against you, you are still Mr or Ms Efficiency at work. Resist the urge to be too bossy, as sometimes your fear of being too direct means you end up being a little bit snappy. And not everyone recognizes how sensitive you are beneath that sometimes cool exterior.

31 THURSDAY

Someone you see on a regular basis, perhaps a colleague at work or just a neighbour, could be a little bit obstinate or difficult today. This is when you need to use all your diplomatic charm, which you have in spades, if only you can recognize it. So take a deep breath, mentally count to ten and speak slowly when you're asking for a favour or giving instructions.

APRIL

Two eclipses enliven what could otherwise be a rather static month for the planets. In fact, only the Sun and Venus actually change signs this month. You could find yourself marking time to a certain extent but, with your vivid imagination, I'm sure you'll be able to utilize this enforced break to visualize the future you would like.

The Sun continues in Aries, the zenith point of your chart, until 19 April. One or two of the irons you have been heating nicely on the fire may be coming to the boil. Remember, you may have to wait just a little bit longer to see the desired results. On 20 April the Sun enters Taurus, the section in your chart linked to club activities, teamwork and friendships in general. Socializing could be a great deal of fun, so you've got nothing to worry about on that score.

Mercury remains in Aries for the entire month, finally

turning direct on 12 April. If you've been waiting to sign on the dotted line, try and postpone it until after this date. Professional projects may get a little boost as well once Mercury is moving in the right direction.

Venus completes the trio of planets in Aries, remaining in that sign until 15 April. If you've been mixing business with pleasure, you may begin to see some rather intriguing developments. On 16 April Venus enters Taurus, throwing a rosy glow over your social life.

Mars continues in Aquarius all month and if you are busy organizing a mortgage or a loan, or going into business with someone, you should have plenty of energy on your side. Remember, however, not to make any firm commitments until after Mercury has turned direct on the 12th.

The New and Full Moons this month are both eclipses, which can be considered catalysts for future action. They are highlighted in the daily guides below.

1 FRIDAY

At the end of the working week, it's traditional to have a drink after work. At least so some people say, and I'm sure if you are invited out this evening, you will have a lovely time. If you have your eye on someone you work with, you can make a big impression now as the planets are all lining up to make you the star of the show.

2 SATURDAY

Your sensitivity helps you to tune in to other people's emotions, which is why you seem to know exactly what to say or do to make your friends and loved ones feel better. Your partner, or someone else close to you, seems to be a little bit down in the dumps and, for once, your sympathy doesn't seem to

be engaged. Perhaps you've been here before and it's getting
a little tedious.

3 SUNDAY

At the moment you seem to be more interested in career matters than your home life. Perhaps this is why certain individuals are behaving in such an irritating manner. It's up to you to
reassure them that your professional plans don't necessarily
exclude their happiness.

4 MONDAY

If you're waiting to sign a contract or a loan or mortgage
agreement, you may find the paperwork arrives today. However, I suggest that you don't sign anything just yet, as there
are some ongoing deceptive planetary links which could confuse matters. Your best course of action is to read and re-read
the small print just to make sure you understand everything.

5 TUESDAY

You love to have your friends and family close by but I'm sure
some of you have relatives and acquaintances scattered
throughout the world. You may hear news from one of them
today, which makes you realize how much you miss his or her
company.

6 WEDNESDAY

With all those exciting plans for your future now, you may be
looking through catalogues for new furniture or fabrics to
make your home the kind of comfortable nest you want. Your
imagination is working very well as usual, but be careful or
you could make a purchase that you come to regret if you are
too impulsive today.

♋

7 THURSDAY

Frustration at work could lead to some frayed tempers and it may be up to you to calm matters down. Friction always upsets your equilibrium but sometimes it's impossible to avoid it. As all those planets are stacked up in fiery Aries, everyone seems to be thinking only of themselves. Someone has to see sense, so perhaps it could be you.

8 FRIDAY

Today there is a New Moon in Aries and it happens to be an eclipse. Recent activities on the work front have made you realize that changes just have to be made before the end of the year. Keep your eyes and ears open and alert today, and you may hear something that you can make good use of later on in the year.

9 SATURDAY

You fancy entertaining at home today but your partner or flat-mates may have other ideas. Unless you are clever and subtle, the result is going to be a miserable stand-off. You're very good at interpreting other people's moods, so why not use this to your advantage?

10 SUNDAY

A spur-of-the-moment invitation could lead to a rather interesting day. Maybe someone you have recently met or don't know very well has thought to include you in his or her plans. I know you are a little shy but this really is a friendship you should follow up; it may turn out to be a very useful connection.

11 MONDAY

There still seems to be a good deal of tension on the work front, and misunderstandings continue to lead to extra work. You may have found yourself again going over paperwork you thought had been dealt with long ago. You just have to be patient and try to keep calm, even though everyone around you is floundering.

12 TUESDAY

Mercury turns direct today and not before time as it has played havoc with paperwork and communications. Of course there may be quite a lot of catching up to do, but the spirit of co-operation seems to have returned after a few weeks' absence. Get together with your colleagues later on and relax.

13 WEDNESDAY

Although contracts and paperwork should run a little more smoothly today please resist committing yourself to any large financial outlays for the next day or so. You may regret it if you agree to a loan or mortgage deal at the moment, as the planets are still encouraging an unrealistic attitude where money is concerned.

14 THURSDAY

You have a wonderful opportunity to impress the boss today. If you've been unemployed for a while and are starting to get a little bit despondent, you need to pull out all the stops today, as the ideal position is right there, waiting for you. Your confidence may have taken a knock recently because of setbacks and disappointments, but you need to put all that behind you as your professional life is just about to take a turn for the better.

15 FRIDAY

Venus is preparing for its move into Taurus tomorrow, a sign where it is very happy. This is also a brilliant position for you as Taurus rules the section of your chart that is linked to friendships and socializing. Not only that, but there is a lovely link between the Moon, currently in your own sign, and unpredictable Uranus, in watery Pisces. Even if you're exhausted, you need to get out there and socialize or you'll regret it.

16 SATURDAY

It may become clear to some of you that your most committed relationship must change or die. Perhaps it was a night out without your partner that made you realize life had more to offer than just a dead-end relationship. I know that it's very hard for you to let go of anything, especially where your emotional security is concerned, but every now and again you have to take a chance.

17 SUNDAY

It's difficult for you to confront emotionally upsetting issues head on. Let's face it, it's difficult for you to confront anything head on, I think you'll agree. Nonetheless sometimes you just have to bite the bullet. You may be surprised at the response you get, as your partner may have one or two complaints of his or her own.

18 MONDAY

Arguments can be very upsetting for you as you do tend to take everything to heart. It is never easy to put your point across if you know it's going to hurt someone. But you do have to stick up for your own values and if you feel taken for granted, in any way at all, you have to speak out.

19 TUESDAY

A routine trip could turn into much more of an adventure today, especially if you lose concentration and find yourself in an unfamiliar neighbourhood. For someone who prefers to stick close to home ground this can be a little bit unsettling, but you might find you rather like it. If you've been hoping to move house, your dream home could be in this new neck of the woods.

20 WEDNESDAY

The Sun follows Venus into Taurus today and those of you not bogged down in arguments with your partner can look forward to a few weeks of happy socializing. Come to think of it, if you are in the middle of such arguments, your friends might provide some support and amusement to take your mind off things.

21 THURSDAY

Your enthusiasm for a new area is either going to inspire your family or irritate them. If it's the latter, you need to try some reverse psychology and at the same time engineer a little diversion for them all. It can't do any harm, can it?

22 FRIDAY

Possibly you've been out and about quite a lot recently and you're looking forward to a quiet night in, enjoying one of your delicious and unusual meals. The perfect follow-up to that is a long hot bath and an early night, hopefully with your sweetheart cuddled up next to you.

23 SATURDAY

Single Crabs may be feeling a little bit lonesome at the moment, but it's really up to you to do something about it, isn't it? After all, the stars are currently working in your favour but you have to put a little bit of effort in as well. If you haven't got anything planned for this evening, get on the phone straightaway and set something up.

24 SUNDAY

There is a Full Moon today in the watery sign of Scorpio. What's more, it is another eclipse. As you know, Scorpio rules the fun and romance section in your chart, so under no circumstances should you sit around at home feeling sorry for yourself. You could be missing out on the chance of a lifetime.

25 MONDAY

Relationships are definitely undergoing changes at the moment. Singles need to be confident and ready to take a chance. Those of you in a long-term partnership may be thinking about where you go from there. If you haven't already decided it's time for change, today's aspects may encourage you to strengthen this particular relationship.

26 TUESDAY

You need to keep your mind focused whatever you're doing today. Any lack of concentration could result in a minor accident, which you really don't need at the moment, do you? We're often tempted to cut corners when doing something that we are familiar with, but every now and again there is a chance it will blow up in our faces, so be careful.

27 WEDNESDAY

It doesn't matter whether you are married with a family or
footloose and fancy-free, there is nothing you like better than
a new household gadget that you can play with. You may find
just the thing today if you're out window-shopping, and you
can't wait to get home and try it out.

28 THURSDAY

If you're a parent, your children could be more a source of
irritation than delight today. A Crab of either sex makes a
devoted parent, as you get such pleasure from watching your
children grow and develop. However if your kids are at the
'why?' stage, even you may be a little bit too tired to answer
every single question.

29 FRIDAY

Your phone could be red hot today and there's no one that
likes a gossip more than you do. If you are at work, you may
have to cut your conversations short though, and even at
home someone else in your household may be fuming that
you are hogging the phone for such long periods. Try and be
fair to others: why not make arrangements to see your friends
face-to-face?

30 SATURDAY

Someone close to you seems to be acting a little bit strange
and this may not be a figment of your own imagination this
time. You never intend to, but occasionally you antagonize
others, possibly because your moods are so unpredictable. In
fact are you sure that you are not a little bit irritable yourself
today?

MAY

The Sun is drifting through earthy Taurus, as usual at this time of year, and your social life will actually be quite busy throughout the month. You may find you are mixing with some rather creative and artistic people who will stimulate your own imagination. On 21 May, the Sun moves into Gemini, which is a rather hidden section of your chart, and you could find you need to spend a bit more time on your own. You know that periods of solitude and contemplation are good for you occasionally.

Mercury is quite busy this month and starts off in Aries. Career matters should be quite positive, and if you're looking for a new job, you need to get your application forms filled in and sent out early on this month. On the 12th, Mercury moves into Taurus. If you're involved in any club activities, someone could ask you to take on a little more responsibility, possibly some administrative duties, which I'm sure you'll find quite easy to slot into your routine. On 28 May, Mercury joins the Sun in Gemini, and you'll be much more interested in working quietly behind the scenes on your own plans and schemes.

Venus begins the month wending its way through Taurus, and it will be attracting all sorts of new and interesting people into your life – assuming that you want it to. On 10 May Venus moves into Gemini, and creative Crabs will have plenty of new ideas, some of which could turn out to be quite lucrative later on in the year.

On May Day, Mars moves into Pisces, the section in your chart linked to foreign affairs, higher education and legal matters. If you're abroad during May, your trip could be more active and stimulating rather than simply relaxing. Lying comatose on the beach may have been your holiday intention but you're much more likely to be exploring all the surrounding areas. Of course, this may even be a business trip rather than a holiday.

On 18 May Neptune, currently in Aquarius, turns retrograde. This is rather a difficult placing for you as Aquarius rules the section in your chart devoted to joint financial responsibilities and assets, and Neptune is a rather deceptive influence. Certain projects that seemed sure-fire winners may have turned out to be complete no-hopers. Worse still, you could have been persuaded to part with your hard-earned cash for some very dubious projects. The very best advice I can give you is to avoid speculation in any shape or form.

1 SUNDAY

Mars moves into Pisces today and as this is a water sign like your good self, Mars here will be a very helpful influence. If you've been feeling rather tired or under the weather lately, you are going to start to perk up. Which is just as well, as you could have quite a few nights out lined up over the weeks to come.

2 MONDAY

Teamwork could be in need of a bit of a shake-up, and if you're in charge you may have to use all your diplomatic skills to make your colleagues understand what you want them to achieve. It's not a question of non-co-operation, but one or two of them don't seem to understand exactly what's required of them.

3 TUESDAY

If you're travelling abroad today, you may find you have a rather special experience. Your sensitivity and intuition help you to absorb the sights, sounds and atmosphere when you're in unfamiliar surroundings. I know that in your world, home is best, but right now you could be enjoying a rather magical moment.

4 WEDNESDAY

Routine matters could be a source of irritation today, and if you aren't one of those lucky Crabs enjoying a taste of the exotic, you may be somewhat grumpy. Try not to take it out on your nearest and dearest because, after all, it isn't really their fault, is it? Why don't you order a takeaway from an exotic restaurant this evening?

5 THURSDAY

Tempers could be fraying both at home and at work, and you may want to lock yourself away in your room and avoid contact with everyone. You know deep down that hiding away under your shell never really achieves anything, don't you? See if you can knock a few heads together and make everyone see some sense.

6 FRIDAY

If you run your own business, you may spot a fantastic window of opportunity that you can sail right through. Your sign's affinity with motherhood ensures that even if you don't have children, your pet projects are treated like your babies. Perhaps this is why you are sometimes in conflict with your partner or family, as you like to have control of every aspect of something.

7 SATURDAY

Single Crabs need to be looking their best this weekend, so if you feel a bit dowdy, why don't you treat yourself to some new clothes or a new hairstyle. The planets are setting up a lovely pattern that may bring somebody rather special on to your scene, and you don't want to miss out on any opportunity to make the right impression, do you?

8 SUNDAY

Today there is a lovely New Moon in Taurus, which gives you the opportunity to make a new set of friends. Of course, you never let go of your old friends, but as far as you're concerned, there's always room for a few more. And now you might be introduced to some people who open your eyes to a whole new world.

9 MONDAY

You're even more receptive to external influences today than normal, and luckily for you everything that's coming your way seems to be positively delightful. It's as if you're seeing the world with a fresh pair of eyes, and any relationship difficulties of the last few months could begin to resolve themselves. Even if you've decided to go it alone, nothing is going to spoil your mood.

10 TUESDAY

Venus moves into Gemini today, where it joins the Moon. You are no less happy than you have been over last few days, but you could require a day or two to process everything that has happened. Hopefully, your family or flatmates will let you have some time to yourself this evening.

11 WEDNESDAY

The conflict between routine responsibilities and space to let your imagination go where it will is a difficult one to resolve. You know that certain aspects of your life need to be kept on the boil but you would like some time to drift and dream. I'm sure you'll be forgiven if you keep a low profile today.

12 THURSDAY

Busy Mercury joins the Sun in Taurus and if you did manage to get a few moments to yourself over the last couple of days, you can pat yourself on the back. The next couple of weeks are likely to be a whirlwind of activity, both socially and, for some of you, professionally.

13 FRIDAY

If someone asks you to take on some extra work, maybe to help out at a club you're involved in, your first response might be to say no. However, if you think about it logically, it can only do your reputation good. And you might meet some different and interesting people.

14 SATURDAY

Why don't you treat your family to a surprise? You've been such a busy bee lately that they may feel a little bit neglected. If you rack your brains, I'm sure you can come up with an idea that will suit everybody and won't be too much of a drain on your wallet.

15 SUNDAY

You could get carried away if you're out shopping today, especially if you see something beautiful that you'd like to have in your own home. While your taste is usually exquisite, in this case you may be slightly off-kilter. If you just have to splash out, for goodness' sake keep the receipt or you will be kicking yourself later on.

16 MONDAY

You may be offered the chance to link up with someone in a foreign country; possibly you have been chosen for a business trip abroad. This could be a catalyst for change in your life in more ways than one, and single Crabs should grab the opportunity with both claws!

17 TUESDAY

You want to tell everyone about your brand-new project and you may be a bit upset if a brother or sister doesn't seem quite so enthusiastic. In fact he or she may appear to be trying to pour cold water over your plans. Have you ever considered that he or she may be just a little bit jealous of your opportunities?

18 WEDNESDAY

You don't take kindly to other people telling you what to do. Although you may not say very much at the time, your method is to agree with them and then carry on in your own fashion. If a member of your family is still trying to get you to see his or her point of view, you're going to have to be very determined, but also very tactful.

19 THURSDAY

Neptune has turned retrograde in Aquarius, and there could be a moment of panic when you open your bank statement or credit-card demand. It's possible you have overspent by rather a wide margin, and you're going to have to exercise some damage limitation quickly. However, if anyone comes to you with a get-rich-quick scheme over the next couple of months, for heaven's sake don't touch it with a barge pole.

20 FRIDAY

The Sun moves into airy Gemini tomorrow, which is a rather secretive section in your chart. You can be a little bit dreamy at the best of times and while the Sun is drifting through this sign, you may become rather absent-minded. You may have to get into the habit of writing lists if there is anything important that you mustn't forget.

21 SATURDAY

Pottering around the house is one of your favourite occupations, I think you'll agree. But other signs just can't understand what it is that is so attractive about housework and moving the furniture around. You just feel a sense of security when all your possessions are close by, don't you?

22 SUNDAY

You may not have been one of the lucky ones chosen to go on a business trip abroad, but today or this evening you could find yourself introduced to a very attractive stranger who happens to come from a foreign country. I know you prefer the familiar but, as I keep telling you, your outlook is changing, so why not give him or her a chance?

23 MONDAY

There is a Full Moon in fiery Sagittarius and perhaps it's because you had rather a late night last night that you are not in the best of tempers. What a shame, as you really haven't had anything to complain about recently, have you? It's true,

though, that without adequate rest you really can be a bit of a
grouch.

24 TUESDAY

If you are getting used to a new routine, whether at work or at
home, this could contribute to feelings of insecurity. You try
hard not to let this sort of thing show but anyone who knows
you well understands that major changes in your routine are
unsettling. Tell yourself that soon you will become accustomed to different working patterns or colleagues and, before
you know it, you will.

25 WEDNESDAY

Someone you work with or see regularly could be a bit difficult to deal with today. Sometimes your instincts let you
down and you may not have noticed that he or she has been a
little bit resentful recently. When we change, some people
can't handle it because they feel threatened. If he or she is
important to you, make a special effort to include them if you
can.

26 THURSDAY

Unresolved partnership issues could raise their head again,
and you may be wishing you were anywhere else but where
you are. Why don't you ring up a close friend and pop out for
a coffee or a bottle of wine that you can share. I'm sure you
have been a great source of support to him or her in the past;
now it's time to turn the tables.

27 FRIDAY

A long-term partnership can stagnate if both partners are not
prepared to keep it alive. All year some of you may have been

wondering whether you'd be better off elsewhere, and a heart-to-heart this evening could make matters clearer – for you at least.

28 SATURDAY

Mercury moves into Gemini, and if you have a lot on your mind you are not going to want to be out there socializing. Sometimes you just need a day or so to process your thoughts. You're ruled mainly by your feelings and sometimes it takes a while to put everything into perspective.

29 SUNDAY

When you love someone you will share your last crust of bread with them, but there is a difference between being generous and being taken for a ride. If you feel that one individual has abused your generosity and goodwill, it's time to call a halt. It doesn't really matter whether this is a member of your family, your lover, a friend or acquaintance. It's time to stand up for yourself.

30 MONDAY

If your weekend was a little bit miserable, just forget it; good news today makes you feel a whole lot better. Unexpected information comes to light, possibly from a friend who's living abroad, or at least quite a way away from you. Why don't you organize a visit? I'm sure you could do with a change of scene.

31 TUESDAY

If you took my advice yesterday and are getting ready for a spontaneous trip, you may find circumstances have conspired to make it a bit difficult for you. Nevertheless, if you really are determined you can easily find someone to water the plants and look after the cat. Don't be put off by a minor setback.

JUNE

If you are a typical Cancer, your home is definitely your castle. You know as well as I do, it's impossible for you to operate to the best of your ability if you don't have a secure and comfortable nest to return to. It's possible one or two of you have decided it's time for change and are gearing yourselves up for the inevitable stress that comes with moving house. You get some extra help this month, as on 6 June Jupiter, currently moving backwards in Libra and the section of your chart linked to the home, turns direct and resumes normal motion. If your plans have been stuck for a while, the opportunity to locate your ideal home may appear within the next couple of months. So you've got nothing to worry about, have you?

Meanwhile, the Sun continues in Gemini and the hidden section of your chart. Keeping a low profile is essential as you gather your strength for all the excitement to come. On 21 June, the Sun moves into your own sign and life should start moving into the fast lane.

Mercury continues breezing through airy Gemini for a few days, until, on 11 June, it enters Cancer. Your little grey cells will be working overtime and you'll be inquisitive and interested in everything that is going on around you. At the end of the month, on the 28th, Mercury pops into Leo. I'll discuss this in more detail next month.

After a few days in Gemini, Venus moves into Cancer on 4 June. Relationships of all kinds will improve if they need to, and, in fact, some will go from strength to strength. If you're a single Cancerian, it's time to get out there and dazzle the opposite sex. On 28 June, Venus also enters Leo.

Mars continues to drift through Pisces and the section of your chart linked to foreign affairs, so you need to be patient if you are dealing with people from abroad. On the 12th, Mars moves into Aries, a sign where it feels very comfortable. This is the zenith point of your chart and career matters may take a turn for the better, although you could have a few disagreements with colleagues. Sometimes you can be a little touchy and if you find others shying away from you, perhaps you need to look at your own attitude.

One more planetary change this month: Uranus, currently in Pisces, decides to start moving in retrograde motion on 14 June. While Uranus is in Pisces, you have an opportunity to change some of your attitudes, especially if you have found yourself stuck in a bit of a rut. Uranus moving retrograde gives you some breathing space in which to review how far you've come.

1 WEDNESDAY

It's time to put on your thinking cap. If you feel as though life has been passing you by somewhat in recent months, there are plenty of changes you can put into place. It's all very well to consider the past, but when you hang on to it too tightly you don't have any room for the future, do you?

2 THURSDAY

If your home life has not been giving you the support you require, you may have been tempted to throw yourself into your career. However, now it's time for you to focus on your domestic needs. While you are in a contemplative frame of mind, why don't you create a picture in your mind of your dream home?

3 FRIDAY

Venus, planet of love, creativity and your value system, moves out of Gemini and into Cancer. You may still be rather quiet, but that doesn't stop you being very attractive to other people. If you've been on the lonely side recently, there is absolutely no need for this state of affairs to continue.

4 SATURDAY

I'm sure you've got plenty of friends who have been wondering where you've been lately, so why don't you pick up that telephone and let them know that you haven't in fact emigrated to the other side of the world? It's surprising to you how much they all seem to have missed you over the last couple of weeks.

5 SUNDAY

Jupiter begins to turn direct in Libra and any quibbles with flatmates or family soon become a thing of the past. If you have been at odds with someone, perhaps about domestic responsibilities, or even whether or not you should or shouldn't move house, everyone seems to be much more willing to discuss matters without getting upset.

6 MONDAY

There is a bright and shiny New Moon in Gemini and you may feel inspired, as this is the section of your chart linked to your subconscious and your secret desires. You are imaginative and intuitive, and any flight of fancy that crosses your mind today could have a real bearing on your future happiness.

7 TUESDAY

Despite your dreamy nature, you're always well aware of the practicalities involved in making major changes to any aspect of life. But don't let these defeat you before you even start. It's the thought that counts, and not just when it comes to giving someone else a present! Perhaps you need to give yourself permission to think big, which is, in fact, the first step on the road to realizing your dreams.

8 WEDNESDAY

You are particularly open today and you shouldn't let grumpy and dissatisfied people affect your mood. Sometimes you're so aware of other people's dissatisfaction that, quite without you knowing it, they can drag you down as well. You have got plenty to look forward to so don't let anyone else spoil it.

9 THURSDAY

Something you hear today or read in the newspaper, or perhaps even see on the television, gives you an idea that you should seize with both hands. It may seem to be very far removed from your current circumstances but once you have given it some thought, it may mean the difference between making do with second best and going for first prize.

10 FRIDAY

The practical side of your nature seems to be taking precedence over the imaginative element. This is very useful when it comes to your immediate responsibilities, but don't let go of any dreams that have recently begun to manifest at the back your mind.

11 SATURDAY

Mercury moves into Cancer and your confidence improves.
You can be very sharp when you need to be, which comes as a
surprise to colleagues and friends alike. In fact your emotional attitude does mask a very astute and shrewd brain,
doesn't it?

12 SUNDAY

Mars changes signs today, moving from dreamy and emotional Pisces to forthright and impulsive Aries. As you know,
this is the zenith point of your chart and if any of you are
nursing some professional ambitions, you may feel somewhat
impatient if you aren't any nearer to achieving them. Mars
now provides you with an extra boost of energy.

13 MONDAY

As far as you're concerned, it's time to turn over a new leaf
professionally, but be careful or you could alienate the very
people you need on your side. Never lose sight of the fact that
you, of all signs, should be guided mainly by your intuition. If
you want to put your case to your boss but don't feel it's the
right moment, hold your horses.

14 TUESDAY

Uranus, that eccentric planet, turns retrograde in Pisces and
the section of your chart which is linked to foreign affairs,
legal matters and a general expansion of your horizons. You
may not realize it but you have changed in a great many
ways, and now you have a chance to reflect on these changes.
I'm sure you've surprised yourself over the last few months,
let alone the people who know you best.

15 WEDNESDAY

If a colleague is acting a little strangely, it is worth considering whether or not you're to blame. Lately you have been quiet and withdrawn and then assertive. You may have inadvertently rubbed someone up the wrong way. Someone has to see sense, so it might as well be you.

16 THURSDAY

Your intuition could lead you to make some progress, especially if you're house hunting. What may seem like a complete no-hoper seems to have grabbed your imagination and you need to convince your partner or flatmates that this is one worth looking at. For once, don't take no for an answer.

17 FRIDAY

You seem to have got out of the wrong side of the bed today, or maybe you just slept badly, but something is bugging you. Your partner, or others whom you live with, are tiptoeing around you in an effort not to upset you. Just because you haven't been able to get your own way, that's no reason to take it out on your nearest and dearest, is it?

18 SATURDAY

In complete contrast to yesterday, you're in a much better frame of mind and ready for anything. If you are a parent, you've got plenty of ideas to keep the kids amused. If you're single, you could meet somebody rather attractive unexpectedly, so for goodness' sake don't just spend the day pottering around at home.

19 SUNDAY

You are probably feeling good today as well, and you are undoubtedly looking great. Try and do something out of the ordinary, or go somewhere you haven't been before. With so many planets in water signs at the moment you really are extremely charismatic, so make the most of it or you will be kicking yourself from here to next week.

20 MONDAY

The boss and your workmates are going to find you a very challenging colleague today. You are an absolute whirlwind of activity and you've got plenty of ideas that you just have to let all and sundry in on. The fact that you are so cheerful with it means that everyone seems to step up to a different level to join you.

21 TUESDAY

The Sun moves into Cancer today, completing the trio of planets in your sign. This is, in a way, the start of your own personal new year, even though it's halfway through everyone else's. Take some time to think about your future plans, both long term and immediate. And why not write down everything you've achieved over the last year while you are about it?

22 WEDNESDAY

There is a Full Moon today and it's in your opposite sign of Capricorn. Have you been so busy with all your own activities that you haven't noticed the tension growing around you? One individual is just about to blow a fuse, if he or she hasn't done so already. You have a choice: you can either step back and help pick up the pieces later, or join in and make it worse.

♋

23 THURSDAY

In the calm after the storm, everyone around you seems to be a little shell-shocked. It's all the more difficult to come to terms with because it was all out of the blue. Or so it seemed. One or two of you, however, may realize that one particular partnership doesn't have much hope of remaining the same. While you are so confident in yourself, this may be the time to end it.

24 FRIDAY

Perhaps your thoughts are turning to what you have shared with someone special over the years. If you're ready to draw a line under a certain relationship, you may be busily doing the sums to see what belongs to whom. However, some of you may have decided to share every part of your life from now on with your partner. If you've chosen this time to get married, the chances are it will be a happy and long-lasting union. The same planetary aspects that pull us apart can also bring us together.

25 SATURDAY

If you're wandering around under a romantic cloud, for goodness' sake don't lose sight of your valuables. While you are in dreamland, unscrupulous types are sharp as a tack and you could find your purse or something else is missing when you reach for it.

26 SUNDAY

If you are emotionally secure, you may now be somewhat twitchy about practical and professional plans. The positions the planets are in at the moment are urging you to reach as high as you can. If you ever wanted to pursue a dream, there is no better time than the present. So long as you maintain a realistic outlook, there is nothing and no one that can stop you.

27 MONDAY

Your head and your heart are in complete and total harmony today and if you've had your eye on someone at work, or someone you just know casually, you could make all the right moves, in the right order. You are always at your best when you listen to your instincts, and at the moment very few can resist you.

28 TUESDAY

Both Mercury and Venus change signs and move into Leo today, the section of your chart representing your money and possessions. Remember this also symbolizes your value system in its entirety, and the concentration of planetary energy in this section may help you to realize that pursuing your dreams is vital to your personal growth and well-being.

29 WEDNESDAY

Your family may expect you to be a bit of a homebody but it's possible you have realized you do have some professional aspirations you want to satisfy. Rather than withdrawing into yourself and sulking, perhaps you should let the people close to you know exactly what it is you want to do. Then you stand a much better chance of getting their support.

30 THURSDAY

You're moving into a period now when your drive and energy is at full power. In actual fact, you can now achieve anything you want to, possibly because you've finally decided to let go of some aspects of your past that have been holding you back. Learn lessons from the past, but don't let it prevent you from moving forwards.

JULY

On 17 July it's time to put out the flags. Saturn, after two and a half years slowly transforming your life, leaves Cancer and enters Leo on that date. Relationships have probably been changed beyond all recognition and while some of you are facing up to life as a single person once again, others of you will be settling down to married life. While Saturn moves through Leo, it's your finances that are going to be under the spotlight. You must take a realistic approach to your money, or you could find yourself tempted to get into debt.

While the Sun is coursing through Cancer, you'll still be functioning at your absolute best. Your optimism is hard to dent and you can achieve a great deal this month. On 23 July the Sun moves into Leo and, bearing in mind that your cash will be uppermost on your agenda, you could start right now by plugging any financial leaks that you notice.

Mercury will be in Leo for the entire month, and on 23 July it turns retrograde again. It's very important that you don't sign any contracts or agreements at this time, especially if they are linked to your money, unless you are absolutely certain they are watertight. You would be far better off waiting until the end of next month.

There is some good news however. Venus is also in Leo for most of the month so there may be a little windfall, or perhaps you remember a little nest egg you've put by that had slipped your mind. Try not to spend it all at once, however, or you could regret it in the months to come. Although there is a great emphasis on your finances there is also the potential to streamline and improve them.

Mars remains in Aries for almost all of July and your career will be thriving. Of course, that is so long as you have remained diplomatic in all your dealings with colleagues and other professional contacts. On 28 July Mars moves into Taurus and, as it remains here until the end of the year, I'll discuss this in greater detail next month.

1 FRIDAY
This month begins with a real sense of potential. You're optimistic about your plans, and even though you know you have several hurdles to leap over, in the long run there is nothing to stop you reaching your goals but your own lack of confidence. And that confidence is growing by the day, don't you agree?

2 SATURDAY
Stay alert today as you may hear something to your advantage. It's possible you could even run into an old friend whom you haven't seen for years. Perhaps this individual has been living overseas or in a different part of the country and has plenty of interesting information that fascinates you.

3 SUNDAY
If you've just moved into a new home, you've got plenty of imaginative and creative ideas about how you want it to look and feel. Window-shopping will provide you with lots of inspiration, and you may even spot the ideal item or colour scheme that feels right for you.

4 MONDAY

If you have a lot of responsibilities or chores to take care of today, you may well have the enthusiasm but not the energy to deal with them. It's important that you don't push yourself too hard or you could find end up feeling a little under par, and that is something you really don't need at the moment.

5 TUESDAY

Don't be despondent if you are in fact feeling a little under the weather. Give yourself permission to relax because, if you do, you may find that new ideas find their way into your mind. Why not relax in a scented bath when you get home from work? After all, water is your element where you feel at your most comfortable.

6 WEDNESDAY

Today is the day of the New Moon and it falls in your sign, which is probably why you have felt the need to withdraw from company to a certain extent recently. New Moons are new beginnings, and when it is in your own sign it could be the start of a fresh cycle in your life. You may come to a decision about an important relationship, and whether it's time to put down some roots or call it a day, you should act on your instincts and not listen to other people's advice.

7 THURSDAY

If you're feeling a little bit isolated emotionally, you need to understand that it is all part of the process. You're coming to the end of one particular cycle in your life and, while not all of you are ready to say goodbye to someone or something that has been important to you, most of you understand deep down that your future is going to be different. It just takes a bit of getting used to.

8 FRIDAY

You feel things very deeply and it sometimes takes you a while to process information that has come your way, especially if it's linked to people you care about. Someone close may disappoint you today and although this is nothing earthshattering, it does shake your confidence a little.

9 SATURDAY

In contrast to the last few days you are feeling much more determined, especially where your money is concerned. This is an inkling of things to come and if your finances are confusing, to say the very least, it's time to get a grip. You could start by making a list of all your outgoings and see which ones can be rearranged to suit you better.

10 SUNDAY

I'm sure you set aside one day a week or, possibly, once a month, to connect with your family. Brothers and sisters are very important to you and you often use them as a sounding board. One of them may have some bright ideas about how to manage your money, so get on the phone right now and pick his or her brains.

11 MONDAY

There may be a surprise in store for you today when you open your front door. Perhaps the postman delivers a package or, more likely, you've got some new neighbours whom you are dying to get to know. For such a home-loving type as yourself, a local network of friends and contacts is essential to make you feel comfortable and secure.

12 TUESDAY

It may take a real effort to drag yourself to work or even to tackle routine chores with any enthusiasm. Unfortunately they won't do themselves, and if you're a parent your children seem to tap into your mood and be about as difficult as they can possibly manage. Resist the temptation to lose your temper, as it will only backfire.

13 WEDNESDAY

Home is where the heart is and you may be longing to get back to where you feel most comfortable. In fact it's you who wants to pamper your loved ones and I'm sure you've bought and prepared some delicious ingredients for dinner. Any recent upsets will soon be forgotten as you relax in this convivial and loving environment.

14 THURSDAY

You have to touch base from time to time in order to achieve your full potential. Now that you realize everyone close to you is on your side, you can make great strides professionally. Over the next few days you're going to be offered plenty of opportunities to increase your responsibilities and your earning potential.

15 FRIDAY

Just because you are firing on all cylinders at work doesn't mean you haven't got time to enjoy yourself as well. It seems at the moment that the more you pack in to life, the more you are going to get out of it. If you're out and about with your friends this evening, you could have a great time, even if it is a little bit expensive.

16 SATURDAY

Saturn is now finally leaving Cancer and moving into Leo. It may be wise to stop a moment and reflect on what changes have occurred in your life over the last couple of years. From now on you're going to have to focus on your material security, and also really come to terms with what is most important to you and what you can let go of.

17 SUNDAY

As if by magic you realize that one obligation is not helpful or useful. Sometimes we carry on in the same old routine without ever stopping to think about how it can be changed. For example, perhaps you joined a gym at the start of the year and have realized that for the last few months you haven't been near the place. Now it's time to cancel your membership.

18 MONDAY

There is no stopping you now as you decide that routines should only be followed so long as they are useful. There is absolutely no point in going through the motions simply because you have always done it this way. You have a chance to change quite a few aspects of your life and though there may be some complaints from your nearest and dearest, you need to stand firm.

19 TUESDAY

If a colleague, or someone you see on a regular basis, is being a bit difficult, it's worth thinking about your behaviour towards him or her. The chances are you may not even like this person, and while you have managed to be charming on a superficial level, your real feelings are apparent without you realizing. You can't like everyone, so be realistic and stop giving yourself a hard time about it.

20 WEDNESDAY

If you spend too much time on your own you can become a little bit cranky, and if you are a single Crab, you need to get out there and make an impression. The next couple of days contain some planetary energy that will link you to other people, so don't stay at home feeling sorry for yourself.

21 THURSDAY

There is a Full Moon in Capricorn, just like there was last month. It's possible your relationship with a colleague or another acquaintance or individual underwent some kind of change last month. Now you may be wondering if you have read too much into this. By the end of the day you're going to have a much clearer picture, so don't get into a panic too early on.

22 FRIDAY

The Sun moves from Cancer to Leo at the weekend, and while you may still be considering all those options, both personally and professionally, you're aware that your finances are in need of some attention. You're very shrewd generally but there's a chance that you have overspent during the last year or so, possibly in an effort to cheer yourself up when things weren't going too well. Now it's time to be realistic.

23 SATURDAY

Venus moves to Virgo, which is the section in your chart linked to close family and your local neighbourhood. You may find yourself mixing with some people introduced to you by a brother or sister or possibly even a neighbour. One individual could flirt shamelessly with you, and unless you're already spoken for, you can enjoy this wholeheartedly.

24 SUNDAY

Yesterday Mercury, currently in Leo, decided to turn retrograde. Remember, this always causes confusion where paperwork is concerned and communications can definitely go haywire. As Leo rules the section of your chart linked to your finances, it's important you don't make any rash decisions for the next three weeks or you could come to regret them.

25 MONDAY

Reality bites and you might get a rude awakening when you open your post this morning. Don't panic, but do resolve to spend this evening going through the figures with a fine-tooth comb. The chances are someone, somewhere has slipped up, but you need to have all the facts at your fingertips before you launch an attack.

26 TUESDAY

Although you may want to spend your time pottering around your home, professional matters need your attention. If you work from home, you could find there is an opportunity that is just too good to miss out on, but it will take a huge amount of time and effort. Don't be put off by this – it could be your big chance.

27 WEDNESDAY

A clash with a colleague could leave a nasty taste in your mouth. It's possible that this individual has been itching to bring you down recently. Rising to the bait may not be the right thing to do, but it's unlikely that you will be able to resist. Someone you know at work will be surprised to see you in such a feisty frame of mind.

28 THURSDAY

Mars moves into Taurus today and the Moon is in Taurus as well, which gives a very sensual and lazy feel to the day. Taurus rules the section of your chart linked to friends, club activities and teamwork of all kinds. This is definitely time to be sociable, but remember to keep your ears and eyes open for information and opportunities to improve your circumstances.

29 FRIDAY

Someone you know, perhaps a colleague, has been looking at you through a fresh pair of eyes. This is very flattering but it is not something you should take very seriously. Although he or she is definitely attracted to you, it looks as though you are really a means to an end.

30 SATURDAY

You end the month on a very thoughtful note. Not only that, but you want to sort out the economics of your situation, and your budget may not stretch to a very extravagant weekend. Never mind, why don't you invite a couple of friends round and share a drink or some food? I'm sure everyone will contribute something if you ask them to.

31 SUNDAY

Sometimes all it needs is a bit of time spent simply being rather than constantly doing. A bright idea crosses your mind today and you may realize that financially matters are not quite as bleak as you had supposed. Run this by your partner or a member of your family, just to make sure you aren't missing some important implications.

AUGUST

August is often a rather lazy and indolent month and 2005 is no exception. There is very little planetary movement and, so long as you watch the pennies, you can have a very relaxing time. The Sun continues to drift through fiery Leo and you will be very sharp, especially when you're out shopping. Although you must be very careful during the second week of the month, as you could lose something you treasure or perhaps get short changed if you don't pay attention. On 23 August the Sun enters Virgo and the section of your chart linked to your brothers and sisters, short journeys and, to a certain extent, your mind and the way you communicate. You'll probably be very busy socializing with your family and there will be plenty to talk about.

Mercury remains in Leo for the entire month, but on 16 August it finally turns direct. If you've been waiting to sign on the dotted line, please try and delay it until after this date or you could be kicking yourself from here to next week.

Venus will be in Virgo for half of the month, ensuring that family get-togethers are great fun. A brother or sister may introduce you to somebody you find rather attractive. On 17 August Venus enters Libra, and your home life will be thriving. If you work from home or make or sell items related to the home, you could be doing rather well.

Mars will be in Taurus all month; in fact it will be in Taurus until the end of the year. This is the section of your chart linked to team and club activities and you may find yourself taking a leading role. Do remember that Mars is a rather aggressive influence and you could clash with an acquaintance or colleague. So long as you are in possession of all the facts, you will not come to any harm, and you could earn yourself some new-found respect into the bargain. This could also bring about some rather steamy contact with attractive members of the opposite sex!

1 MONDAY

Although you may find it hard to drag yourself out of bed today, you'll be glad when you do. There is a very sociable atmosphere today and you should make the most of it. But under no circumstances part with a large sum of money or you could regret it.

2 TUESDAY

A familiar journey could turn into a magical mystery tour and you may find your thoughts wandering. This is when you can bump into people quite by chance who turn out to have a profound influence on your life. So if someone approaches you, don't run away.

3 WEDNESDAY

If you happen to be on holiday, perhaps in a foreign country, enjoy yourself but try not to over-indulge. If you have too much to drink you might find you end up penniless, which would be a real shame, don't you agree?

4 THURSDAY

There are plenty of things you can do to amuse yourself that don't cost a lot of money, and if you are a parent, the kids as well. After all, you are one of the most imaginative signs in the Zodiac and I'm sure that you can keep everybody happy without breaking the bank if you put your mind to it. I know pester power is the bane of many a parent's life but there are other ways to entertain the little dears.

5 FRIDAY

There is a New Moon in Leo today, and you may find just the opportunity you've been looking for to make a bit of extra cash. You will probably hear about this through a friend or neighbour, and if it's local, so much the better, as you really don't want to spend too much time commuting at the moment.

6 SATURDAY

You are very enthusiastic about all your new plans and can't wait to tell your partner or family about them. Unfortunately someone seems to have the wrong end of the stick and assumes that this means you are going to be working every hour of the day, and possibly some of the night as well. You may need to reassure him or her that this is not the case.

7 SUNDAY

Entertaining at home is a lovely way to spend today, especially if your family are close at hand and can join you. If the weather's nice why don't you try a barbecue? I'm sure everyone will be pleased to join in and lend a hand. It doesn't have to be perfect and you can all have a bit of a laugh.

8 MONDAY

You probably received plenty of compliments about your hospitality over the weekend but the chances are you're feeling a little jaded now. Most of the time you concentrate on making other people feel happy and comfortable so it's about time you did something for yourself. You could visit the hairdresser for a change of look.

9 TUESDAY

Be very careful if you're out shopping as you may find you are attracted to something that is way beyond your budget at the moment. We all know that there are plenty of enticing deals that allow you to pay gradually, but right now is not the time to sign up for one of them. You need to be clear headed if you're about to commit yourself and today's aspects are not really favourable.

10 WEDNESDAY

Perhaps you realize that you don't need that item that seemed so desirable yesterday. If it was for the home, a little bit of imagination could give you exactly the same effect. In fact you're so creative at the moment that you are turning your home into a bit of a showplace. Don't forget it must be comfortable first and foremost.

11 THURSDAY

If you're in love, you may be filled with a sudden desire to let your partner know exactly how you feel. Of course this is fine if you've been together for a long time and you are in tune with each other's moods and feelings. However, if this is a new affair, it might be best if you hold your tongue just a little longer.

12 FRIDAY

Socializing could be a sparky affair tonight, and if you are footloose and fancy-free you may find yourself falling under the spell of a sexy stranger. This may not be Mr or Ms Right, but if your flirtation muscles have been under-used lately, they can at least get a little bit of welcome exercise.

13 SATURDAY

This is turning into rather an intriguing weekend, especially if you're single. One of your friends may introduce you to somebody who seems to be an ideal companion. Don't get too carried away, but don't be too cool, calm and collected either!

14 SUNDAY

If you've been wading through a pile of paperwork over the last few weeks you will be keen to see the light at the end of the tunnel. Financial affairs need to be put into some kind of order if you're going to survive Saturn's transit to the money-bags section of your chart in the coming week. You'll be very glad if you've taken the time to do this.

15 MONDAY

A female colleague could be rather difficult and while you may be racking your brains to figure out why, the chances are it's purely and simply jealousy. After all, over the last month you have been the centre of attention from time to time, and some people just can't cope with being sidelined, even for a short while.

16 TUESDAY

You might get a flurry of phone calls today as Mercury, currently Leo, turns around and starts moving in the right direction again. If you've been waiting to sign on the dotted line, perhaps a new job contract or even a mortgage, it just might arrive in the post this morning.

17 WEDNESDAY

Sympathetic Venus moves into Libra and the section of your chart devoted to your home and family. You are always happiest when your domestic situation is running smoothly, and life is definitely going to improve if there have been any difficulties with flatmates or your partner lately.

18 THURSDAY

If you're moving house, you are probably very excited about the prospect. At the moment the planetary set-up is ideal for decorating and choosing fabrics and colours. It's important, however, that you act as though you are still on an economic shoestring, at least for the time being, otherwise you could throw good money after bad during the next few days.

19 FRIDAY

There is a Full Moon today in the eccentric and detached sign of Aquarius. This is the section of your chart linked not only to financial considerations but also to sharing on an intimate level. You're such an emotional person that, if you aren't careful, other people's eccentric behaviour could be very wounding. Take a leaf out of the Aquarian book and remain detached from other people's emotions.

20 SATURDAY

You could be feeling rather restless and edgy today and it's worth considering why this is. While security is important for you, there is also a growing need to expand your horizons.

Regardless of your age, the need for personal growth may be tempting you to think about higher education of some kind. Don't dismiss this as a whim.

21 SUNDAY

You may be looking forward to an evening with your friends but it's possible that, rather than feeling comfortable with them, you feel a sense of alienation. Remember that you're going through some major changes in your outlook and it's worth considering if some of your old friends are still compatible with your new ideas.

22 MONDAY

If you work from home, you must seize every opportunity that comes your way today. You may feel a bit overloaded and wish there were a lot more hours in the day, but now you've got a chance to make some important connections that will help you build up your business and raise your profile.

23 TUESDAY

The Sun enters Virgo today and your little grey cells are beginning to perk up. If you work in the media or your job involves communications with the public, you could be rather busy. In fact you are likely to feel exhausted by the end of the day, so do try to relax or you could find yourself feeling below par all week.

24 WEDNESDAY

Learning to let go is something Saturn has taught you over the last few years, and if you are wondering why you're still involved with one particular circle of acquaintances or club, you may get confirmation today that it's time for a change.

25 THURSDAY

A clash with a friend or colleague might leave you feeling rather unsettled. You may find it hard to understand or accept that sometimes it's actually down to you. Your sensitivity is such that sometimes you respond to slights that never existed in the first place. In this instance someone has to see sense, so why shouldn't it be you?

26 FRIDAY

Perhaps you have withdrawn into your shell to lick your wounds. You do take things very much to heart, which is why you get the wrong end of the stick so often. You might need to talk over recent events with somebody close, perhaps a brother or sister, who could help you get everything back into proportion.

27 SATURDAY

The boot seems to be on the other foot today as someone close to you is feeling a bit down in the dumps. Of course, this is when you really come into your own, and you will be fussing around him or her like a mother hen. There is nothing you like more than mothering people who mean a lot to you, is there?

28 SUNDAY

Routine chores could be very irritating today, as everything seems to take so much longer than you anticipate. If you can't get someone to help you, perhaps you should give yourself permission to take a break. Sometimes leaving things to settle makes it easier to deal with them later on.

29 MONDAY

In contrast to the weekend, you are feeling a lot more yourself today. Instead of seeking out the familiar, you're looking for something different. Perhaps a phone call or a letter from family or friends abroad has stimulated your desire to see more of the world. If you haven't been on holiday yet, perhaps you can get a last-minute bargain.

30 TUESDAY

You are firing on all cylinders and your grey matter is absolutely on top form. Sometimes we have days when we really believe that anything is possible, and this could be one of them in your case. Don't let anyone bring you down or spoil your plans.

31 WEDNESDAY

If you're counting the pennies, perhaps in order to book a long-distance holiday, you may be a little bit alarmed at the state of your finances. There always seems to be so much less than we think, doesn't there? Well I'm sure you can find a way around this difficult situation if you put your mind to it.

SEPTEMBER

Routine matters and your relationships with co-workers have been undergoing subtle change over the last few years. Pluto, the planet of transformation, has been moving through Sagittarius and the routine and sheer hard slog section of your chart. Recently it's been moving in retrograde, but on 3 September it turns direct again. You will understand why one individual has been so difficult to get along with. Now you have a chance to overcome this and stop it bothering you.

As usual during the first part of September, the Sun will be in Virgo, and you have plenty of opportunity to catch up with your family. You may even decide it's time to go into business with a brother or sister. On 23 September, the Sun moves into Libra and your home life becomes paramount. If you're a freelancer, you will have plenty of opportunities to expand your business.

Mercury spends a just a few days in Leo this month, and on the 5th it too enters earthy Virgo. You could find a meeting or club locally that interests you and if it stimulates your brain cells as well, so much the better. On 21 September Mercury enters Libra, and it's a good time to catch up on domestic paperwork. I'm sure there are several important documents that you have hidden away and forgotten about.

Venus continues in Libra, throwing a rosy glow over your home life. Your imagination could help you to use limited resources to make your home a palace. On 12 September Venus enters Scorpio, a water sign like your good self. This is the section of your chart devoted to the good times, and you will be the star of the show socially. If you're a parent your children could be little angels, which, I'm sure you'll agree, is very uncharacteristic. So make the most of it!

Mars continues to move through earthy Taurus and you may surprise others as you become more assertive in clubs and teams that you're involved with. Socially, you may also take the lead and you must be prepared for one or two individuals to respond negatively. However, this could also be a very sensual and sexy time for you, so if you're single please don't be shy.

1 THURSDAY

When you've been at odds with a colleague, sometimes the hardest thing to do is open up a dialogue. This is what you must do right now even if it only confirms your suspicions that he or she is not really someone you can count on your side. Surely it's better to know than continue to wonder, isn't it?

2 FRIDAY

Pluto is turning direct in Sagittarius now, and the section of your chart linked to sheer hard slog. It's possible that new working practices or even a new job mean you have had to change your routines and also your attitude. But, in contrast to the past, you're now much happier to do so.

3 SATURDAY

There is a lovely New Moon in clever and diligent Virgo. If you've recently moved house you are going to be exploring your new neighbourhood with interest. Your grey cells are all on red alert at the moment, and you'll find that the information you need comes to you easily, making decisions a cinch.

4 SUNDAY

With Mercury about to move into Virgo your curiosity and interest is enhanced. Socializing has to be more than just a drink or meal today, and you might organize your friends and family into a team in the local pub quiz. You may even decide that you want to explore a local museum or art gallery.

5 MONDAY

Home is where the heart is, but if you have been feeling slightly resentful that a flatmate is not pulling his or her weight you might decide to tackle this issue today. The planets are all on your side, and you'll find it easier than usual to say exactly what you want to. No one is under any illusions that you are going to be a domestic doormat any more.

6 TUESDAY

A quiet night in might be what you are expecting this evening but there very well could be surprise visitors arriving on your doorstep. You may be a little bit taken aback at first and panic if you haven't got enough food and drink to satisfy everyone. Don't worry: you are so hospitable they won't even notice and, anyway, it's you they've come to visit.

7 WEDNESDAY

A new relationship could move on to a much more intimate footing now and perhaps you have organized a candlelit romantic dinner for two. Sometimes you can be a bit shy, but don't be frightened to take the lead this time around. Your intuition has led you to this point and I'm sure that it's right.

8 THURSDAY

Single Crabs should be on the lookout for attractive strangers over the next couple of days. If you haven't arranged any evenings out socializing, do it right away. However mundane the surroundings, you're in the right place at the right time to meet someone special. And there's nothing like the prospect of winter just around the corner to make you long for some love, is there?

9 FRIDAY

There could be some real sparks flying if you've met someone you fancy recently. Once your emotions are engaged, you can become an incredibly sensual person – not at all the shy and strait-laced image you often present to the outside world, don't you agree?

10 SATURDAY

If you are wandering around with a rather secretive smile on your face, your friends may be very interested to hear your news. If I were you, I would keep my thoughts to myself, as not everyone is really as generous hearted as they pretend to be. There is nothing like jealousy rearing its ugly head to spoil the day.

11 SUNDAY

Resentment and jealousy are emotions you find very hard to deal with. The truth is, we all harbour these feelings from time to time, and once we recognize this, it is easier to handle other people's emotions. Don't let the behaviour of a friend or acquaintance upset you, as you are on course for a rather special few weeks.

12 MONDAY

Venus moves into Scorpio and you really are a sexy beast at the moment. If you met someone way back in April who pushed all the right buttons, he or she could return to your life over the next few weeks. Regardless of this, you must make sure your diary is filled with events where you can mix with new people on a grand scale.

13 TUESDAY

Your phone will be constantly ringing, both at work and at home, and if you are too busy to talk you may end up with a list of people to ring back. At home, your partner or flatmates may be getting a little bit hot under the collar if you hog the telephone all night, so do try to be fair about it, won't you?

14 WEDNESDAY

Relationships can so often be damaged by arguments about money and if you're in a long-term partnership, beware that your other half may have very different ideas about how you should spend your joint assets. Of course when it comes to money you are pretty shrewd, but once in a while you can be a bit misguided, so don't dig your heels in too deep.

15 THURSDAY

You may be all of a dither if you've just met somebody that intrigues you. You may be sharing confidences this evening, which opens up the possibility of this relationship growing stronger. Remember to listen to what he or she is saying without putting your own spin on it, so that you are certain to get the real message that is being put across.

16 FRIDAY

You may have fallen completely under someone's spell and hopefully he or she is not spinning you a line. Deep down you're very romantic, and also very generous hearted, so by all means enjoy this relationship but don't be too keen to show how much you care just yet. Remember, at the moment you are very alluring and it's a good idea to keep your options open for just a little while longer.

17 SATURDAY

A friend or member of your family may suggest something completely out of the ordinary today. You'll be thrilled and won't even mind travelling quite a long distance as you really fancy a change. You may have your work cut out making sure the kids are entertained during the trip, if you have them, but in the end it will all be worth it.

18 SUNDAY

There is a Full Moon in emotional Pisces today and tempers may be a little bit on edge. I'm sure it's probably because everyone is a bit tired and it's important you all give each other some space in which to relax. You might even fancy going off on your own at some point, just so that you can blow all the cobwebs away.

19 MONDAY

You could be mixing business with pleasure today and you might meet someone who has an interest in you that goes far beyond your professional skills and capabilities. It seems that at the moment you are beating them off with a stick. This is a wonderful position to find yourself in, isn't it?

20 TUESDAY

You could be puzzled by the behaviour of a friend or acquaintance, but remember, jealousy and resentment are never far from the surface. If he or she has been used to you following other people's leads, it may come as a shock when you express a few ideas of your own. Don't be put off; it isn't your problem.

21 WEDNESDAY

Mercury moves into Libra and those of you who are self-employed or who make or sell items for the home need to get your thinking caps on. There is plenty of scope to improve your business but you have to put in some effort. Use your intuition together with your practical skills and your business will soon be thriving.

22 THURSDAY

By the end of today you'll probably be longing to get home for some solitude. It's not that you don't want to see anyone, but you need some time to process your thoughts. Cook yourself a lovely meal, have a long bath and an early night, and you will be raring to go by tomorrow morning.

23 FRIDAY

The Sun moves to Libra and the section of your chart linked not only to your home but also to your most intimate thoughts and feelings. With its kindly rays shining a light into your soul, you may discover that certain feelings you were afraid of are actually incredibly valuable. While it's true that your relationships are undergoing a certain amount of change, it seems as though it's all for the better.

24 SATURDAY

If your home is in a mess, it can't help but unsettle you. Before you even think of hitting the town, perhaps you need to tidy up a few of your things. Mindless and routine chores can be quite soothing when you've got a lot to think about, and you'll be very happy later on with your spotless and comfortable home.

25 SUNDAY

You can be forgiven for being a little dreamy and absent minded today. It seems for many of you, your love-life is a source of pleasure rather than confusion at the moment. Try not to think too far ahead; just enjoy the moment.

26 MONDAY

Being back in the old routine is something you'd rather forgo, if the truth be told. Never mind, at least one of your colleagues can be trusted to listen to you without judging you. Even if someone in your circle is hoping that you'll fall flat on your face, you don't have to give him or her that pleasure do you?

27 TUESDAY

There is such a peculiar mix of planetary activity today that you may end up feeling rather confused. While some people are firmly on your side, others seem to be determined to bring you down. Still others act like they are rooting for you, but deep down you suspect their motives. This is one day to definitely keep your thoughts to yourself.

28 WEDNESDAY

It's a relief to concentrate on practical and financial matters. Whether these are your own personal concerns or something to do with work is irrelevant. You can put all your suspicions about other people to one side and get on with the job quietly and in your own time.

29 THURSDAY

Sometimes you just have to take a chance in life, and one individual who has recently come to mean a great deal to you may ask you to do just that. Perhaps he or she has suggested a long-distance trip, which fills you by turns with fear and excitement. Wait a few more days before you make your decision.

30 FRIDAY

Talking over a current dilemma with a brother or sister may seem obvious but in fact it could leave you more confused than before. This time you need to rely solely on your own judgement. As your outlook has changed over the last year or so, your confidence has also grown. So why are you so unsure now?

OCTOBER

This is an action-packed month as far as the planets are concerned. Not only is there all the regular movement of the stars but there are two eclipses to contend with. They occur in Libra and Aries and will affect both your home life and your working practices.

The Sun continues to drift through Libra and your home is certainly the focus of much of your attention. Remember that Jupiter remains in Libra until the end of the month and any changes you want to make at home will benefit from Jupiter in this position. So try and put anything new into place before the end of the month. On 23 October the Sun moves into Scorpio, and anything you do for pleasure should be thriving.

Mercury visits three signs this month, starting in Libra. On 9 October the planet moves to watery Scorpio and your hobbies may take on a more intellectual tinge. You may not be going for a PhD but you'll probably be enjoying crossword puzzles and word games. If you've got children you can combine entertainment with learning. At the end of the month, on the 30th, Mercury moves to Sagittarius and the sheer hard slog section of your chart. Things will start to get pretty busy.

Venus spends another week in Scorpio, so make the most of her sensual influence. On 8 October Venus moves to

Sagittarius, which is the health and beauty section in your chart. You may be tempted to over-indulge, especially if the days are getting cooler, but you can also use Venus' influence to improve your appearance. Which is it going to be?

Mars continues in Taurus all month, but on the first day it turns retrograde. Taurus rules the section of your chart linked to friendships and team and club activities, and you may have grown used to being in charge to a certain extent while Mars has been moving through this sign. Now that it has turned retrograde for couple of months, you can expect to be challenged on more than one occasion if you start throwing your weight around. And you may also find you have to retrace your steps, as a project that you thought was finished may need some more tinkering with.

I've already mentioned Jupiter and it's important this month because it changes signs. On 26 October it will enter Scorpio. As you know, this section is linked to romance among other things, and as Jupiter is the planet of opportunity you've got lots to look forward to. You've probably already had a taste of all the fun that is going to come your way over the next year.

There's one other planetary change to mention, as Neptune turns direct after several months moving backwards in Aquarius, on the 27th. As this is one of the money sections in your chart you may realize that some of your decisions have not been to your advantage. Without being too impulsive, perhaps you should try and reverse some of these decisions.

1 SATURDAY

The month begins with Mars turning retrograde, for reasons best known to itself, and it's impact may be felt straight away. The chances are that a social engagement with your friends that has been in place for a while is cancelled, or perhaps several people pull out at the last minute. It's no good getting cross about this, you just have to accept it.

2 SUNDAY

You may be feeling a little put out as you were hoping to run into someone you've had your eye on for a while yesterday. Well, if this is something that is meant to be, nothing is going to prevent it, so calm down and be patient. The weekend doesn't have to be a complete washout; you could always invite a friend round and cook one of your lovely meals.

3 MONDAY

Today's New Moon in Libra is in eclipse and it falls in the section of your chart to linked to your home and family. Eclipses are often connected to dramatic changes, and while it's often not apparent at the time, shifts in relationships could become more important later. Perhaps you've decided on an unconscious level that it's time to move on.

4 TUESDAY

It's essential you allow your instincts to guide you today in whatever you're doing. If you feel nervous about tackling a delicate issue with a colleague or uneasy when you're in an unfamiliar neighbourhood, don't try and rationalize it away. Act on your gut feelings.

5 WEDNESDAY

Sometimes the planets conspire to put you in the right place at the right time, and if you've had a crush on someone you only know slightly, he or she may be about to enter your life rather more. Even if the one whom you have your eye on doesn't show up, it seems as though a little flirtation is definitely on the cards.

6 THURSDAY

You can sometimes be a bit moody, which leads your nearest and dearest to tear their hair out from time to time. You may wake up this morning rather grouchy and if you continue in this fashion you're going to miss out on some rather interesting opportunities. If you're tired of being lonely, you really had better work that frown off your face and start smiling.

7 FRIDAY

It's true that you are a creature of habit, but you may come up with an innovation today that you just can't ignore. Don't be shy about letting your colleagues in on your secret, as they will be delighted to help you put your new idea into practice. Sometimes you are too frightened to speak up for yourself but this really is something you must learn to do.

8 SATURDAY

Both Mercury and Venus change signs this weekend so it could be one full of surprises. Venus moves from watery Scorpio into fiery Sagittarius today. Don't be too despondent now that Venus has left your house of fun – Mercury moves in to replace it tomorrow. I'm sure you'll be busy chatting with your friends and making plans for this evening.

9 SUNDAY

Your love of food is legendary and it's possible you are having trouble squeezing into some of your favourite clothes. If this is the case, don't you think it's time that you took a long, hard look at your attitude to your body? It might be a good idea to give yourself a bit of a makeover before the party season.

10 MONDAY

Your phone could be red hot today, and if you have to share it with others perhaps you should be a bit more considerate. Once you get an idea in your head, you want to let all and sundry know about it. In fact gossip and Cancer go together like gin and tonic, don't you agree? But the latter are off the menu if you are slimming!

11 TUESDAY

It seems that you've inspired all your friends and everyone is as keen as you to get into shape. Of course exercise is also one of the ways we can improve our health and slim down a little, but as this is really not your sort of thing, it's essential that you convince your mates to join you down at the gym or the swimming pool.

12 WEDNESDAY

If you're considering taking out a loan and purchasing something expensive such as a car, it might be a good idea to wait for a few days. Planetary aspects at the moment are not conducive to getting a good deal, and you hate to be ripped off or short-changed in any way, don't you?

13 THURSDAY

You might get chatting to someone new, perhaps on the bus or at the supermarket, who has a very intriguing take on life. This could set you thinking, especially if you feel as though you have been in a bit of a rut lately. You know intuitively that certain aspects of your working life really do have to change, even though you may have forced this to the back of your mind through the summer.

14 FRIDAY

You've got plenty to talk about with your partner or your family but bear in mind that others often prefer us to remain exactly as we are. If you feel you want to spread your wings a little, it's vital that you reassure loved ones that it doesn't mean you are going to fly too far away.

15 SATURDAY

If you've recently become involved with someone new, prepare yourself for a surprise at some point over the weekend. It may be that he or she has decided not to take this any further. However, it could equally be a charming gesture that makes you feel cherished and adored.

16 SUNDAY

This may be a day of rest but your little grey cells are working their socks off. If you've decided that before the end of the year you're going to make some professional changes, the chances are you're boring anyone within earshot about your new ideas. It might be better to keep them to yourself until they are clearer.

17 MONDAY

Today there is a Full Moon in fiery Aries, which is at the zenith point of your chart. It is also an eclipse, which can be a catalyst for dramatic events. A disagreement with a colleague or frustration at your current line of work could boil over at some point, leaving you either screaming your head off or in

floods of tears. It's bound to calm down, but you should
remember what it was that brought you to this point.

18 TUESDAY

If you're in need of some TLC, you should meet up with some
friends who have nothing to do with your work. You want to
be with some sympathetic people with broad shoulders that
you can cry on. The chances are someone will have some very
good advice for you as well.

19 WEDNESDAY

The Moon and Mars link up today and I'm afraid it looks like
more frustration for you. Teamwork is likely to be difficult
and if you happen to be the leader of the pack, it may be an
uphill struggle to get everyone to see your point of view. If
this has happened before it could be another indication it's
time for you to move on.

20 THURSDAY

You may still be smarting from yesterday's exchanges and
you will want to keep a bit of a low profile. This doesn't prevent your mind working overtime and you should keep a pen
and notepad handy to jot down any of your ideas. Remember,
when one thing comes to an end it leaves a lovely clear space
for something new to appear.

21 FRIDAY

It's not all bad news this week, as a chance for a little bit of
undercover flirtation has reared its head. Hopefully neither of
you has someone waiting patiently at home. However, this is
too potent for you to ignore it, so just be very, very careful.

22 SATURDAY

When you want to hide something, you can look as though butter wouldn't melt in your mouth. If someone at home is a little suspicious, they may well have very good grounds. Perhaps you ought to think about how you would feel if the boot were on the other foot.

23 SUNDAY

The Sun moves from airy Libra to watery Scorpio, and so far this month has proved to be one of many highs and lows. Now that there is a watery feel to the planets, you are much more in harmony with your environment. Arguments may still occur but you are less unsettled by them than you were.

24 MONDAY

The atmosphere at work will be much more conducive to harmonious relations with your colleagues. You could find yourself chatting away happily to someone who you wanted to kill last week. It just goes to show that it is all a question of how you look at things, doesn't it? But you might still be considering the possibility of a change of job.

25 TUESDAY

You can be a bit of a hoarder; in fact your house is probably a bit like a museum. It's not really the right time of year for spring-cleaning but it might be quite useful now, especially if you're thinking of making some personal or professional changes. Sometimes the simple act of cleaning out cupboards allows new ideas to manifest themselves.

26 WEDNESDAY

Jupiter, the planet that brings opportunities and luck into our lives, changes signs today after spending the past year in Libra. Your home life feels much more settled and Jupiter now turns its attention to your love life, your children and your creativity. For a whole year this helpful planet is going to be in Scorpio, encouraging you to take risks and enjoy yourself.

27 THURSDAY

Neptune, after several months backtracking through Aquarius, turns direct and resumes normal motion. This is in the big-business and joint finances section in your chart, and you may have to sort out a mess that you have created with your assets. Hopefully this is not too dramatic and you will be able to get back on track, as long as you remain realistic.

28 FRIDAY

You may be starting as you mean to go on, but if you put too many petty restrictions on your spending, you are only going to drive yourself mad. You just need to be sensible, especially where large amounts of money are concerned. Your instincts are usually right, but it's always wise before you commit yourself financially to get a second opinion.

29 SATURDAY

Brothers or sisters could be the ones to go for if you need a little bit of advice, as it seems at least one of them appears to be very astute. Of course you won't be talking about money all the time, as I'm sure there are plenty of other topics you can cover during the course of a leisurely meal or a quiet drink.

30 SUNDAY

Mercury, the communications planet, moves into fiery Sagittarius today. This is the sheer hard slog section of your chart as well as the health and beauty section. If you're worried about your waistline, it may be helpful to read up about a new diet before you embark on your fitness regime.

31 MONDAY

If you're footloose and fancy-free, perhaps you need a change of outlook. Your sensitivity can sometimes make you too shy to initiate a conversation and it also puts up an invisible barrier to other people. Tell yourself that you have nothing to fear by making the first move, and over the next month or so you are going to be beating them off with a stick.

NOVEMBER

The Sun is still drifting through watery Scorpio and it is throwing a rosy glow over your love life, your children and, in fact, anything you do that gives you pleasure. You may decide to try and market your creativity if you paint, write or make things as a hobby. On 22 November the Sun enters Sagittarius, and you will be rushing around, hither and thither, organizing the festivities to come.

Mercury will be in Sagittarius for most of the month but on 14 November it turns retrograde, as it so often does. Bear in mind at this busy time of year that communications are liable to get scrambled and short journeys can turn into marathons. By 26 November, Mercury will have moved so far back it re-enters Scorpio. Any unfinished business linked to a casual relationship may reappear. Perhaps you'll have the chance to put things right this time.

Venus starts off in Sagittarius and on 5 November it moves into your opposite number Capricorn. This is a lovely position for you, as all relationships, not only those that are close up and personal, go through a golden phase. Remember, Jupiter is also in a romantic section of your chart, so you could be looking at a fantastic end to the year.

Mars continues moving backwards through Taurus and this could be the only fly in the ointment. Some relationships with professional contacts or teams or clubs you're involved with could be a little fraught. Remember to be diplomatic and the chances are you'll manage to get your own way.

Saturn and Uranus both change direction this month. Saturn, in Leo and the section of your chart linked to possessions and money, turns retrograde on 22 November. If you've been struggling with your finances, you will now have some welcome respite. Uranus in Pisces has been backtracking for a few months and turns direct on the 16th. This is a nice end to the year, as this planetary placement is encouraging you to make long-term plans. You may surprise your friends and loved ones with your ideas but don't be deterred by anyone.

1 TUESDAY

There is a very mixed feel to the planets today and the atmosphere is bubbling under with mystery. Although you may have plenty on your plate, it's very difficult for you to concentrate, and if you can delegate some of the more frustrating chores I suggest that you do so.

2 WEDNESDAY

There is a New Moon in Scorpio, which may be why you felt so on edge yesterday. As you know, New Moons often mean new beginnings and one relationship that has been rather casual may take a step forward. It's important that you are honest about your feelings, with yourself, as well as your opposite number.

3 THURSDAY
Socializing could be very expensive at the moment, and you may have to forgo one particular pleasure because your pennies just won't stretch as far as you would like. It's a shame, but I'm sure you'd rather have plenty of cash to see you through the coming month rather than having to scrimp and save, wouldn't you?

4 FRIDAY
If you are typical of your sign, you will start stashing away goodies for Christmas as early as now. After all, food is one of your greatest pleasures and there is nothing like knowing you have all the ingredients you need to make the festivities go with the swing. Try not to sample the goods – especially if you want to lose a bit of weight.

5 SATURDAY
Venus moves into your opposite number of Capricorn and I'm sure your partner, if you have one, is letting you know exactly how fabulous you are. What about single Crabs? I know you hate to be all on your ownsome and you can be sure that over the next few weeks there are going to be plenty of opportunities to meet attractive members of the opposite sex who push all the right buttons for you.

6 SUNDAY
It's not only your partner but also your friends who seem to want to be around you at the moment. You are always

happiest when the people you love are happy as well and some of your famous hospitality today could ensure that this is the case.

7 MONDAY

A colleague may have been very difficult recently and in your usual fashion you might assume it's all your fault. Today you may have a flash of insight that helps you to understand why he or she has been so uncommunicative. Take this opportunity to show him or her that you care and you will be very glad that you did.

8 TUESDAY

You could be surprised to find someone is flirting with you completely out of the blue. This person has never shown the slightest interest in you and you may feel slightly uneasy. I'm always telling you to go with your instincts, and in this case it may be that he or she is not being completely open with you. It's very sad but some people seem to think it's OK to use others for their own ends.

9 WEDNESDAY

Don't waste time thinking about yesterday's events. You've got plenty of other fish to fry and you may come up with rather an intriguing scheme to cut your workload without losing out financially. If you're a homemaker you may get some real bargains if you're quick off the mark.

10 THURSDAY

Like most of us, you've probably got friends and family scattered all over the place, and the chances are someone is going to be thinking about you today. You may intuitively know that this is happening and phone or e-mail on your own initiative. It's bitter-sweet, as you enjoy the conversation but are sad that it isn't face to face.

11 FRIDAY
Some lucky Crabs will be packing their bags for a romantic weekend away. I know that you prefer to be on home ground as it makes you feel more secure, but just for once, why not stop worrying? You seem to be on course for a lovely weekend, so sit back and enjoy it.

12 SATURDAY
If this is just a routine Saturday for you and you haven't been whisked away, you may find yourself in a rather grumpy frame of mind. In fact the planets are conspiring to give you the courage to change certain aspects of your life. Rather than repressing these feelings of frustration, try and use them constructively.

13 SUNDAY
You could feel as though you're marking time today as hundreds of different thoughts are vying to become uppermost in your mind. Obviously something has been stirred up, but you aren't going to be able to make use of it unless you put your thoughts in some kind of order. Write down everything, however unimportant it seems, and then you can assess it all later on.

14 MONDAY
Mercury turns retrograde again today and routine matters become a real quagmire. It doesn't matter whether you are at college, at work or at home, nothing is going to run smoothly.

Of course you can't just give up, but it's in your interests to prioritize and leave the less important matters until you have more time for them.

15 TUESDAY

Uranus, currently in Pisces, is about to start moving in the right direction again after several months in retrograde motion. This section of your chart is linked to legal affairs, foreign travel and higher education. If you're involved in a legal matter, new information could come to light soon, which might change the course of events.

16 WEDNESDAY

There is a Full Moon today in the earthy and stubborn sign of Taurus. You could find one of your friends is being rather obstinate, but rather than dig your heels in too, a step back and a healthy sense of humour will get you through this tricky moment. After all, you really don't want to fall out with anyone at this time of year, do you?

17 THURSDAY

Someone close to you may be rather sheepish today but don't be tempted to rub salt in the wound. If you act as though nothing serious has happened, you will soon be back on good terms. You're really not in the mood to hold a grudge at the moment.

18 FRIDAY

Many people suffer from light-related seasonal depression at this time of year, and as a summer-born sign this often happens to you. However, this particular year you may have a wonderful sense of optimism, especially if you have just met someone whom you feel may become rather special. Hold tight to this thought.

19 SATURDAY
Your buoyant mood continues into the weekend. You're beginning to understand the logic behind the cliché about how we make our own luck. For someone who has so often been subject to gloomy moods, this is a very different state of affairs, which you could quite easily get used to.

20 SUNDAY
Regardless of whether or not you have children, your instinct for nurturing others is never far away. Perhaps you want to gather some friends and family together for a leisurely meal. If you know someone who's on their own at the moment, you could invite him or her along as well. The gesture will really be appreciated.

21 MONDAY
Resist the temptation to get into a panic if your bank balance is looking a bit thin. It's true that your finances have been a bit of a black shadow at the back of your mind over the last couple of months. However, your determination to retain your security ensures that nothing too disastrous is going to happen to you. Try and cultivate a little bit of detachment and clear thinking.

22 TUESDAY
The Sun moves into fiery Sagittarius today, which is the sheer hard slog section in your chart. Not only are you going to continue to be rushed off your feet at work, but I'm sure you are making numerous plans for the coming holiday season too.

For goodness' sake, schedule in some time to simply sit and dream or you will get overtired.

23 WEDNESDAY

Yesterday, mighty Saturn decided to start moving in retrograde motion. Saturn is the reality planet in astrology, and as it is now in Leo and the section of your chart devoted to your money and possessions, it is encouraging you to face facts. You have already realized that certain economic changes need to be made. Now you have some breathing space, which you should use carefully.

24 THURSDAY

An unexpected cry for help from one of your family may upset your plans for today. The chances are that there is nothing very much to worry about but he or she does seem to be taking it all rather seriously. Bear in mind this could just be a way of getting your attention.

25 FRIDAY

The extra work caused by this sudden problem in your family may have left you a little bit behind schedule. With Mercury backtracking in the routine section of your chart recently you've probably not even made a dent in the mountain of tasks you have set yourself. A few moments spent dividing up what's essential from what can wait will take a load off your mind.

26 SATURDAY

Mercury has moved so far back it's returned to Scorpio and the romance section of your chart. You always have trouble letting go, especially when an affair has ended unexpectedly.

Unfinished business is something you find very troubling, so stay alert over the next week and you might finally be able to see the full picture.

27 SUNDAY
Children can be a real handful at this time of year, and if you're a parent you'll probably be gearing up to tell one or two fibs simply to keep them quiet. The planetary aspects currently in place indicate that your little dears are not going to be fobbed off with any old story. You're going to have to be really clever if you want to keep all your secrets.

28 MONDAY
Some gossip you overhear today could be quite unsettling, especially if it relates to someone you care about. You may think that there is no smoke without fire but sometimes other people are simply malicious. Before you wade in, wait until you have all the facts at your disposal.

29 TUESDAY
A female colleague may really have pushed you a little bit too far. Everyone tends to be stressed out at this time of year, and while it's not like you to go on the offensive, this time you're not going to be anyone's doormat, are you? Your response now will make this individual think twice before attacking you again.

30 WEDNESDAY
If you hear from an ex partner sometime today you may be rather puzzled by what he or she has to say to you. It's worth giving it some thought before you respond, as you could realize you have been under a misapprehension about why things

went wrong between you. It doesn't necessarily mean this relationship will be resurrected, but it does make you feel a bit better about it.

DECEMBER

This December there are two New Moons, which are both significant in your chart. Remember, New Moons indicate the chance for new beginnings, and there is nothing better at the close of the year than the prospect of something new to look forward to later on in the coming year.

Meanwhile the Sun continues in Sagittarius, and you are going to be running yourself ragged making certain that all those lovely little touches are in place to make your Christmas very special. The chances are you will be the host, as this is your forte, isn't it? On 22 December, the Sun moves to your opposite number Capricorn, ensuring that plenty of people are going to want to be close to you. Not only are your loved ones going to be gathered around you, but also friends and acquaintances from all those different areas of your life.

Mercury begins the month retrograde in Scorpio until 4 December, when it turns direct and social activities and communications will run smoothly once again. On the 13th Mercury moves back into Sagittarius, which means that the Christmas post should all arrive on time!

Venus starts December in your opposite number Capricorn. It's really rotten being single at this time of year but you now have Venus on your side if you're hoping to meet someone special to share the festivities with. You are going to be looking good and feeling great, so you've got nothing to worry about, have you? On 16 December Venus enters Aquarius and you may be lucky enough to receive a little windfall –

just at the time you probably need it most. However, Venus turns retrograde on Christmas Eve, and some presents may have to be returned to the shop; for goodness' sake keep the receipts, won't you? I'll let you into a secret now: as Venus is moving retrograde it will be back in Capricorn in January, giving you a second bite of any romantic cherry you missed the first time around.

Energetic Mars continues all month in Taurus, and while it remains retrograde for the first few days, on 10 December it finally turns direct. This gives a further boost to your social life, so there is no reason for you to be sitting at home, twiddling your thumbs and watching TV, is there?

1 THURSDAY

What better way to start the month than with a brand New Moon? This one is in fiery Sagittarius and the section of your chart linked to routine matters, professional relationships and your health. If you have been baffled by a difficult relationship with a colleague, you have an opportunity to make a fresh start now. Why not hold out the olive branch and see what happens?

2 FRIDAY

It may take quite an effort on your part to persuade a colleague but you really are willing to bury the hatchet. This person seems to have a great many problems of his or her own, which is probably why he or she seems so hard to get to know. If anyone can do it, I'm sure you can.

3 SATURDAY

This could be a fantastically busy period as we run up to the festive season. Today you seem to be in great demand, and you may have to let someone down. I'm sure you'll be as kind and considerate as you possibly can but it might be an idea to arrange to meet another day immediately.

4 SUNDAY

Mercury turns direct today, in the sign of Scorpio. If ghosts from the past have been troubling you recently, you have an opportunity now to lay them to rest. Sometimes we really do just have to put bad experiences behind us. However upsetting it has been recently, try and look at it as part of your own personal growth.

5 MONDAY

The last thing you need at this time of year is unnecessary expense, and if you're involved in a team or club you may be wondering whether it's really something you can afford. Of course, as always, you have trouble backing out of commitments because you hate to let others down. Remember, the most important thing about your own financial stability is that you are realistic, and if something has to go, it just has to go.

6 TUESDAY

I'm sure you want to do the best for your children, if you have them, but if the money just won't stretch to all that expensive computer gear they all seem to want, then it simply won't stretch, will it? A little bit of imagination could mean that you keep them happy and don't break the bank.

7 WEDNESDAY

I am sure you are longing to hear from your friends and relatives scattered throughout the world. The chances are that,

now communications are running much more smoothly,
you're going to hear from one of them today. It's always sad
when you know you're not going to see loved ones in the
immediate future but at least you know they're thinking of
you, just as you are thinking of them.

8 THURSDAY

You can make great strides with routine matters today as long
as you keep focused. Of course this is always quite hard for
you as you do sometimes drift off into La La Land, don't you?
This is one of your personality traits that others find quite
endearing; however, occasionally it can knock you off-course.

9 FRIDAY

If you work outside the home, I'm sure you are absolutely
determined to clear your desk as soon as possible. This is particularly important if you've decided that next year you're
going to embark on a new career. It's not like you to do anything less than your absolute best but don't completely
exhaust yourself. Remember, there only so many hours in the
day.

10 SATURDAY

Mars finally turns direct today after what seems like ages
moving backwards in the sign of Taurus. This section of your
chart links to team and club activities, and friendships and
socializing in general. There may have been one or two
instances over the last couple of months when you felt at odds
with people who usually make you feel comfortable. Now
Mars is moving in the right direction you are confident that
anyone you have lost contact with is no great loss.

☙

11 SUNDAY
What starts out as a purely social occasion could have reper-
cussions on your professional future. Someone you meet at a
party or club may be able to put you in touch with exactly the
right contacts you need to further your ambitions. It's hard
not to babble on about this but please don't bore your partner
or family.

12 MONDAY
There is a lovely earthy feel to the relationship sections in
your chart, and you realize that while some individuals have
disappeared from your circle, the ones whom you value the
most are still here, large as life. If you have one or two glasses
of wine you may come over all sentimental. But then, that's
why they all love you, isn't it?

13 TUESDAY
Now Mercury is on the right lines again, it moves back into
Sagittarius today, affecting the routine section of your chart.
You can breathe a huge sigh of relief as all those obstacles
you've been facing recently while going about your daily
business seem to have melted away as if by magic. But don't
take on anything extra, please.

14 WEDNESDAY
We're approaching a Full Moon and everyone seems to be in a
complete tizzy as deadlines are looming and there just seems
to be too much to do. You are always affected by the tension
in the atmosphere and may unwittingly be swept along by the
general stress. Try to remain detached from it all.

15 THURSDAY

Well, today's Full Moon in Gemini is here, and it links up with the difficult planet Pluto. If you've managed to keep your head, all well and good; however, your sensitive nature could mean that you have reacted more than everyone else. You may need to apologize to someone if you bit his or her head off.

16 FRIDAY

Venus drifts into airy Aquarius, which is the sign ruling the section of your chart linked to joint financial assets and responsibilities. Be on the lookout for a small windfall over the next few days. This section also links up to sharing on an intimate scale, and you could be looking forward to getting home to your partner for some of that TLC you badly need after recent upsets.

17 SATURDAY

It's just as well we've reached the weekend as you could be feeling as though you've been torn to pieces. Don't waste time worrying about who said what. Everyone is a little bit over-sensitive and touchy when stressed out. You can easily make amends on Monday, perhaps by taking a box of chocolates into the office.

18 SUNDAY

You may be rushing around looking for last-minute bargains, so do be very careful with your money in the crowd. And please remember to keep all those receipts somewhere safe, as the chances of something being wrong with one of your gifts, however well chosen, are very high.

19 MONDAY

There could be a rather quiet atmosphere at work, especially if there was a great deal of shenanigans on Friday. You're very good at making others feel relaxed, so use all your talents to make your colleagues feel comfortable with each other before the holidays.

20 TUESDAY

You are very shrewd and believe firmly that if you look after the pennies the pounds will look after themselves. If you are out shopping today, you could pick up more than one excellent bargain, especially if it's food. Your mouth is probably watering on the way home with the thought of all your goodies stashed away safely.

21 WEDNESDAY

The Sun begins to move into Capricorn, and because you're so determined to have everything organized, you may be the one person who is able to relax a little bit. You also seem to have a whole army of helpers determined to take some of the weight off your shoulders. Just occasionally you can be a bit of a control freak, but right now you need to let your helpers get on with things.

22 THURSDAY

Perhaps you ignored yesterday's advice, and if you find yourself being a bit of a bossy boots, especially in the kitchen, you could run the risk of spoiling the atmosphere. I know you are a perfectionist and no one is able to do things quite the way you do, but surely it's the thought that counts, isn't it?

23 FRIDAY

It may be your last day at work, and you're going to make a massive effort to leave a good impression. If your colleagues accuse you of being a goody-two-shoes, don't let your sensitivity push you off-course. Be reasonable: they are bound to tease you at this time of year because no one really has their mind on their work, do they? But it's important for your future, and you aren't going to lose sight of your precious professional goals.

24 SATURDAY

Well, it's Christmas Eve, and you seem to have made a monumental effort to get everything organized. Now you can sit back and survey the scene with a great deal of satisfaction. Perhaps you are even enjoying a few glasses of wine with your partner or friends. Venus, planet of love and all good things, turns retrograde today, so remember not to take it to heart if some of your gifts don't quite hit the spot tomorrow.

25 SUNDAY

HAPPY CHRISTMAS! The big day is finally here, and to make matters even better for you, the Moon is sitting firmly in Libra and the section of your chart linked to home and family. I'm sure you'll be rushing around making sure everybody has exactly what they need, and while it's tiring, it's something you love doing, if the truth be told. You're bound to have a wonderful time.

26 MONDAY

Boxing Day is always a bit more laid-back and you often find unexpected visitors knocking on your door. In fact, the planets have arranged it so that this Boxing Day is incredibly sociable; knowing you, the cupboards are groaning with drink and the fridge is bursting with food. The best part of this time of year is feeding all your friends and making them feel warm and comfortable, isn't it?

27 TUESDAY

You still seem to be at the centre of a social whirl, and single Crabs are going to be looking around for someone to pamper. Well, with the Sun in your opposite number you're certainly going to be in great demand, so just relax and enjoy yourself.

28 WEDNESDAY

You are a real bargain hunter and you may be itching to get out there and join in with the throng at the winter sales. Remember, if you don't need it, it's not a bargain, regardless of how cheap it is! Your financial situation could be a lot better, so unless you're absolutely in dire need, try and resist the shops.

29 THURSDAY

If friends and family are still lounging around at home you might like to enlist them in a bit of a clear-up. Once you have decided it's time to sweep up all those needles from under the tree and make sure all that left-over food is disposed of, no one and nothing is going to get in your way. Some members of your family are going to be making a beeline for the pub today!

30 FRIDAY

Your phone is likely to be constantly off the hook, and if you haven't yet decided exactly how you're going to welcome in 2006 there are bound to be plenty of options for you to choose from. If you're single, use your intuition to guide you, and make it one of your New Year resolutions that this is how you're going to plan your future from now on.

31 SATURDAY

Well, New Year's Eve is finally here, and as if to really put the icing on the cake, there is a brand New Moon in your opposite sign of Capricorn. If you're spending this evening with your partner you'll have a fabulous time as you realize just how much you mean to each other. Single Crabs also have a lot to look forward to, as a New Moon in your opposite sign is a clear indication of the potential for a new relationship. So dress yourself up to the nines and get out there and sparkle!

HAPPY NEW YEAR!

Your Birth Chart
by Teri King

A Book of Life

Simply fill in your details on the form below for an interpretation of your birth chart compiled by TERI KING. Your birth chart will be supplied bound and personalized. Each chart costs £40.00 Sterling – add £2.50 Sterling for postage if you live outside the UK (US Dollars are not accepted). Cheques should be made payable to *Kingstar* and sent together with your form to: PO Box 3444, Brighton, East Sussex, BN1 4BX, England. For all *Kingstar* enquiries contact bright77_@hotmail.com.

Date of Birth _____ Place of Birth _____

Time of Birth _____

Country of Birth _____

Name (in BLOCK CAPITALS) _____

Address _____

_____

_____ Postcode _____

Email _____

A birth chart makes an ideal present. On a seperate sheet, why not include the details of a friend, partner or a member of your family? Please see the above costs for each individual chart.

Do you know someone who has difficulty reading normal print?

If you are experiencing medical sighted difficulties, the National Recording Service provides 200 national and international magazines and newspapers in both audio and electronic format in the United Kingdom.

For further information on subscriptions, contact:

The Talking Newspaper Association
National Recording Centre
Heathfield
East Sussex
TN21 8DB

Telephone: 0870 442 9590
Email: info@tnauk.org.uk